Migrations, Arts and Postcoloniality in the Mediterranean

This book is focused on the transcultural memory of the Mediterranean region and the different ways it is articulated by contemporary art practices and museum projects linked to migration, exile, diaspora and transnationality. The artistic and curatorial examples analysed in this study articulate a critical relationship between the cultural representations and the sense of heritage, property and belonging, offering the opportunity of a more problematic and stimulating vision of the preservation of the European arts, traditions and histories. Artists and projects examined include the project *Porto M* in Lampedusa, Zineb Sedira, Ursula Biemann, Lara Baladi, Mona Hatoum, Emily Jacir, Kader Attia and Walid Raad.

Celeste Ianniciello is an independent researcher and member of the Centre for Postcolonial and Gender Studies, University of Naples "L'Orientale".

Routledge Focus on Art History and Visual Studies

1   Advancing a Different Modernism
    SA Mansbach

Migrations, Arts and Postcoloniality in the Mediterranean

Celeste Ianniciello

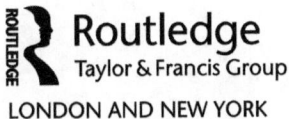

Routledge
Taylor & Francis Group

LONDON AND NEW YORK

First published 2018 by Routledge

2 Park Square, Milton Park, Abingdon, Oxon OX14 4RN
605 Third Avenue, New York, NY 10017

Routledge is an imprint of the Taylor & Francis Group, an informa business

First issued in paperback 2021

Library of Congress Cataloging-in-Publication Data
Names: Ianniciello, Celeste, author.
Title: Migrations, arts and postcoloniality in the Mediterranean /
    Celeste Ianniciello.
Description: New York : Routledge, 2018. | Includes bibliographical
    references and index.
Identifiers: LCCN 2018017167 | ISBN 9781138479609 (hardback) |
    ISBN 9781351061933 (adobe) | ISBN 9781351061926 (epub) |
    ISBN 9781351061919 (mobi)
Subjects: LCSH: Mediterranean Region—In art. | Memory in art. |
    Postcolonialism and the arts.
Classification: LCC N8214.5.M48 I23 2018 | DDC 700.9/045—dc23
LC record available at https://lccn.loc.gov/2018017167

ISBN: 978-1-138-47960-9 (hbk)
ISBN: 978-1-03-217871-4 (pbk)
DOI: 10.4324/9781351061940

Typeset in Sabon
by Apex CoVantage, LLC

Contents

Illustrations

Introduction

The book is focused on the transcultural memory of the Mediterranean region and the different ways it is articulated by contemporary art practices and museum projects linked to migration, exile, diaspora and transnationality. The work's main theme is the analysis of how some innovative artistic and curatorial projects propose alternative visions and practices of memorialising and archiving the past, evidencing the multiple connections between the past and the contemporary postcolonial configuration of the world.

In this analysis the different case-studies, which emerged as a result of both individual research (carried out within the PhD in Cultural and Postcolonial Studies of the Anglophone World, at the University of Naples "L'Orientale") and as part of group field research (carried out within the MeLa* European research project about the rethinking of European museums and archives in the light of global processes of migration), are intimately interlaced because they all propose a critical reflection on the complex and layered interconnection between the different cultural, economic, historical, geographical and social contexts of contemporary Europe and world. Thus, particular attention is paid to the Mediterranean area, recognising in the global processes of migration and in their historical formation a fundamental element for understanding the present.

In this sense, the artistic and curatorial practices emerging from experiences of migration and cultural hybridity are not understood simply as objects of political and social analysis but rather in terms of active practices of processes of becoming, able to question the forms and canons, exploring the relationship between difference and identity, the geographical locations and dislocations, the borders and cultural displacements, through a dynamics of constant contamination and reciprocal resignification between art and theory, as for example Bracha Lichtenberg Ettingher indicates:

> The work of art does not illustrate or establish theory; theory can only partly cover – uncover – the work of art. Sometimes the work of art produces seeds of theory from which, upon elaboration, art slips away. These seeds should be sown somewhere else. The most graceful moments in the covenant between art and theory can occur when theoretical elements, only indirectly or partly intended for particular works of art, and visual elements that refuse theory, collide. In doing so they transform the borderline between the two domains, so that art is momentarily touched by theory while theory takes on a new meaning.
>
> (Ettinger 1993, 11)

The artistic and curatorial examples analysed in this study articulate a critical relationship between cultural representations and the sense of heritage, property and belonging, offering the opportunity of a more problematic and stimulating vision of the preservation of European arts, traditions and history. The dimension of processuality and the theoretical, practical and cultural becoming that characterises the works analysed here are connected to an innovative and experimental use of digital technology and the critical possibilities inscribed in synesthetic and sensorial images and their power to act upon and affect bodies.

In this perspective, images can be understood not simply as representations of reality, but rather as life themselves, producers of new senses and meanings. This allows us to highlight the relations between aesthetic languages and political practices, with their different modes of actualisation and intervention, especially considered from the critical perspective of postcolonial studies. In fact, my research has adopted an interdisciplinary approach that unites sociology, history, anthropology and philosophy to critical and artistic analysis. Particular importance has been given to the radical theoretical and aesthetic contributions coming from feminist and feminine productions.

The book highlights how some contemporary postcolonial art practices and curatorial projects emerging from the Mediterranean area and directly linked to experiences of migration open up the possibility of activating alternative memories, in opposition to the current nationalist maps and institutions of power and knowledge, as they have been defined by the cultural and political economy of Occidental colonialism. The aim of the present work is to emphasise how art is able to create zones of ontological slippage, spatio-temporal interlacing, contact zones between collective and personal memory, critical intersections between global and local, proximate and distant, proper and improper, self and other. Interrogating our position, our habitual procedures of recognition and definition, art transposes us into a critical space, beyond the visible, under the "peel" of domesticated time, in a region not delimited by frontiers, closeness, division, but signed by traces, folds, movements, unpredictable currents, migrations of bodies and senses.

The book is divided into three main chapters, each of which is composed of four subchapters. The first chapter, "Frames: Spaces and Borders, Transits and Positionings", proposes an analysis of the complex relationship between place, territory, cartography, geography and the sense of belonging, the space of property and identity, the places of the self and personal territory through the critical perspective of feminist theory and female aesthetics. In this discourse it is shown how the autobiographical genre, first in the literary form then in the visual one, assumes particular cultural and political relief, above all if it concerns female migrant subjectivities. Aesthetic feminist/female discourses and languages, in particular those able to create alliances, relationships or connections, such as the collage, are understood as critical counter-narratives and counter-visions of nationalist and monoculturalist culture and of the politics of border surveillance, which has characterised the European and national politics of migration in the last decades.

The second chapter, "Narrations: Transcultural Memories and Migrations", tries to trace a common line with the critical instances of the previous chapter in contrast with nationalist logic – its politics and institutional apparatuses, its culture and epistemology – through an analysis of the museum: considered traditionally as the place where national memory is conserved and preserved. This chapter highlights how what has been defined as the "national museum" can be questioned and rethought in the future terms of a "postcolonial museum". This possibility of museum, archival and memorial reconfiguration arises from some curatorial practices and aesthetics emerging from the Mediterranean region, such as the project *Porto M* in Lampedusa; the artistic productions of the Algerian artist Zineb Sedira; and the videocartographic researches of the Swiss artist Ursula Biemann, through which the Mediterranean is registered as an archive of border-crossings, contaminations, fluid and intersected memories, the liquid residence of a migrant modernity. This part concludes with a focus on the research project, *The Matri-Archive of the Mediterranean*, about the archiving and circulation of contemporary artworks produced by female artists from the Mediterranean region. Particular attention is paid here to an art project based in Naples, *The Land of the Overseas Territories* by Alessandra Cianelli, which opens up the archives of Italian colonial history, taking the artist's family memories as a starting point.

The last chapter, "Installations: Heritage, Belonging and Out-of-Place Legacies", is dedicated to a series of case-studies through which the relationship between historical, geographical and identitarian belonging, citizenship and property, heritage and material and immaterial patrimony is discussed. In particular, the chapter focuses on the diverse innovative and critical forms and articulations of this relationship in the Egyptian–Lebanese artist Lara Baladi's art of nomadism and progressive transformation; the Lebanese–Palestinian artist Mona Hatoum's art of displacement and defamiliarisation of domesticity; the Palestinian artist Emily Jacir's art of active participation and cultural reappropriation; and the French–Algerian artist Kader Attia's and the Lebanese artist Walid Raad's art of error, disturbance, damage and simultaneously of reparation, re-memberment and incessant re-creation.

1 Frames
Spaces and Borders, Transits and Positionings

The Geography of Barriers and the Politics of Patrol

This chapter explores the relationship between space, borders, transits and placement and directly investigates the possibility of exploring geography as a field of knowledge. In addition, it questions its disciplining power, along with the strategies and mechanisms that sustain it, which are based essentially on visibility. The formation of geography as the knowledge of spatial reality is founded on territorial borders and the possibility of defining reality itself through the delimitation of space and the mapping of territories. Therefore the role of the visual power of the subject can be considered a structural historical element. This is the organic premise from which Occidental Enlightenment epistemology was born, developing into the biopolitical culture of today. It consists, as Michel Foucault reminds us, of a correspondence between seeing, knowing and exercising power (see Foucault [1967]; Senellart 2007). In the West, the territorial knowledge and power derived from practices of visualizing reality are historically linked. Cartography emerges and develops as a science with the expansion and development of imperialism and colonial conquests. A disciplining knowledge and a hegemonic power are here interlaced, reflecting the coeval humanist vision of knowledge. This is based on principles of neutrality, objectivity and abstraction guaranteed by a dominant, disembodied and universal subject. Thus, in the relationships between mapping and defining the world, those connections between sight, knowledge and dominance are also inscribed: "However objective they may appear, maps do have a point of view, and that is one of privileged super-human sight, of safe distance and of omniscience. The mapmaker charts an entire field of vision, an entire world, and in doing so he (yes he) plays God" (Fusco 2004). This is a white man's vision, subjected ultimately to a will of framing aimed at the stabilisation of fixed territorial identities. A vision that germinated within the imperialist, colonialist and patriarchal system and that even today does not give up its grasp on the world, persisting in the current Occidental nationalist culture and politics (Diagne 2013).

The production of borders and the obsession for what we could define as a "geography of fortifications" has dominated Europe's political agenda for decades and can now be also considered a global phenomenon. As Wendy Brown points out, the border has become the material institution through which the declining power of the nation-state seeks to defend its presumed integrity against what are perceived as external menaces coming from contemporary reality: terrorists, poverty, epidemic viruses and, above all, poor migrants (Brown 2010). Walls of separation proliferate all over the world in order to fortify and defend the nations, showing instead how national borders are porous and fragile. We see examples of these walls of concrete and barbed wire, cameras and technological sensors, in militarized checkpoints between Mexico and the United States, India and Pakistan, Egypt and Gaza, South Africa and Zimbabwe, Saudi Arabia and Yemen, in Europe, on the Spanish borders in Morocco, on the eastern border of Hungary, in Macedonia, in the Mediterranean Sea between Libya and Lampedusa.

In the age where the global fluxes of migration have gained the strongest intensification ever, borderlands are paradoxically turned into spaces of containment, regimes of arrest and immobility. The Italian scholar Sandro Mezzadra defines today's frontiers as the space of bio-power and "tanatopolitics", a space where state power exercises control over migrant people through capitalist dynamics of inclusion/exclusion based on the erection and patrolling of borders which results in death (Mezzadra 2008). This is the result of what Mezzadra, echoing William Walters (2004), defines as "domopolitics". The definition indicates the necessity to protect "home" (*domus*), coinciding with the will to dominate (*dominus*) and at the same time domesticate, evoking the etymological proximity between *domus* and *dominus*. The result is a correspondence between possessing or occupying a domain and exercising dominion, or the relationship between property and power. Both the concepts of "tanatopolitics" and "domopolitics" are strictly connected to colonial power and the concept of "necropolitics" elaborated by Achille Mbembe (2008). Mbembe highlights the fundamental racist trait and the lethal dominion over bodies inscribed within those politics. In fact, until recently, European politics, as Mezzadra explains, aimed at turning migrants from ungovernable fluxes into governable subjects of functional mobility responding to the national economic exigencies of the work-force. Now, Europe has pushed even further its inhuman logic of exploitation with the politics of rejection that send migrants to their deaths. This has contributed to xenophobic and islamophobic anxieties unhinged by recent terroristic attacks subsequently obtaining electoral consent. As Ida Dominjanni writes: "the whole most atrocious weight of European history precipitates on the so-called migratory emergence, with the ineluctable ferociousness of a return of the repressed: as the traces of its tanatopolitics of extermination materialised again in the bodies of people asphyxiated in the tracks or in the ship cargos; in the corpses buried in the sea, and even in the taxonomic rationality of Angela Merkel, who opens the doors to the Syrian refugees, but only to them" (Dominjanni 2015).

In this extreme defence against the (colonial) repressed, the European obsession with borders, other than attesting a connivance with neo-liberal dictates, combines with the necessity to affirm its cultural hegemony through a patriotic, nationalist, racist rhetoric. This is what happened, as Judith Butler explains, with the mainstream public islamophobic discourse of the post-9/11 United States, in the wars against Iraq and Afghanistan. Similarly, today's European nation-states are engaged in strategies of representation and communication aimed at a cultural and identitarian homogenization. This is done through an emphasis on individualism and an ostentation of a pervasively masculinist, strong, sovereign (male) subject, able to defend his identity and way of life. Thus, following this logic from a neo-liberal perspective, a migrant woman coming from Arab Africa represents a body – or, better, a single unit of the work-force – on which to exercise the power of selection and exclusion. From the perspective of the dominant cultural discourse, she represents a "foreign body" to be tolerated or integrated into the social tissue in the best cases but more and more widely to be refused and expelled.

Precisely at a moment of radical crisis for Occidental economic, cultural and political sovereignty, the ideology of the "same" re-emerges obliquely and substantially in Europe. At the centre of this crisis lies faith in identity, authoritarian and centralized power, and securitarian, militarist and fascist politics. Europe seems to persist in the lethal mistake of considering itself the centre of the world. Like a divine eye that sees from above, this translates to measuring and deciding, establishing a presumably universalistic – but actually colonial and exclusivist – vision, which perpetuates its ontological imperialism. Thirty years ago, questioning the monoculturalist and instrumental assumptions about the national identity of the British subject, and hence European cultural identity, Paul Gilroy asked if it was possible to consider blacks or Muslims as Europeans. This brought attention to the inadequacy of the nationalist stance against the complexity of contemporary society (Gilroy 1987). Similarly for citizenship, what is the legal status of the multiple cultural belongings of the Muslim immigrants and their children born and raised in Europe? Gilroy's critique is even more implacably problematic if we consider all those subjects living in juridical and civic limbo, such as refugees and asylum seekers. In the persisting void of adequate responses, a clear will persists in opportunistically framing the varied "in between" subjects as "marginal others". Still today, the critical instances of postcolonial discourse have to register a refusal or an inability to understand the different experiences of migration beyond a colonial or patriotic logic or, alternatively, humanitarian rhetoric.

Such conditions of displacement as migration, exile, expropriation and border-crossing could also be considered other than solely experiences of loss, domination and appropriation. It is possible to think of the border(land) as other than the place where people die, where life stops. On the contrary, borderlands can be considered as the critical spaces of renovation and transformation, where a rethinking of the horizons of the proper, of property, of identity and of belonging can take place. It is possible to undermine and rewrite the deadening cartography of the limits, which Western power has drawn and continues to define. Geography can be thus understood as a process of spatialisation given by the multiple occupation of spaces, reflecting on the ways subjects locate and dislocate and, as Judith Butler suggests (2004), considering their vulnerability. This opens up the possibility of overcoming the distance between a dominant and universal subject, who sees and defines the world, and the world as a void space waiting to be defined and appropriated. As Irit Rogoff underlines, geography could be then better understood in its relation to the contemporary contest of visual culture, where visibilities and invisibilities, power relations and stereotypes are both regulated and contrasted (2000).

Engaging the visual as an interdisciplinary and fluid interpretative frame, it is possible to debate and contest the social interactions of racialised identities, gender and class. As Stuart Hall stresses in *Visual Culture* (Hall and Evans 1999), the question of how to imagine visual culture is concerned with the cultural practices of looking and seeing and the capacity of images to produce meaning. However, since these meanings cannot be completed within the text, their realisation requires the subjective capacities of the viewer to make images signify. As Frantz Fanon highlights in *Black Skin, White Masks* ([1952]), the question of the gaze is crucial for the production of the identity of the subaltern subject, because it is through the power of the gaze that

Fanon understands himself as a black subaltern subject, as an object among other objects.

At the end of the 1999s, when the field of visual culture studies came to be defined very clearly by Nicholas Mirzoeff (1998; 1999), the visual became a cultural phenomenon, included in a more general politics of representation, since the image is essentially a place of creation of meanings. Mirzoeff analyses the interactions between the viewer-as-subject and the viewed object that trigger the production and the circulation of images. Visuality is thus developed as a problematic domain, where it is possible to rethink the formation of power as a visualised model on a global scale and the place of subjects within that system, in other words, people defined both as the agents of sight and as the objects of particular regimes of visuality. In particular, this interconnection leads to the very specificity of the images that confront the new and emerging conditions of multicultural societies. The dimension of visuality as a critical tool for thinking about questions of citizenship, belonging and identity is especially evident in artistic examples emerging from both sensorial and imagined experiences of geographical and cultural passages: migration, diaspora, transculturation and creolisation, which actually bring us into the contemporary, that is the interstitial temporality of our world.

The artistic productions and processes presented here evoke the autobiographical experience of transit and migration across different lands, languages, cultures, sounds, flavours, and stories. Separation of space from time, geography from history, present from past, here from elsewhere seems impossible within these experiences. These productions propose a constant personal and collective translation, producing alternative cartographies of memory and belonging, redefining both one's own and the other's space and identity. What is here described as postcolonial art, in an epistemological sense as well as in a historical and geographical perspective, offers the possibility of an alternative narration, or a counter-narration, of the world and the self, whose genealogy germinates within the feminist critical thought and its situated knowledge.

Border-Crossings: Feminisms and the Bodies of Knowledge

Against a colonial vision of the world, subjectivity and difference, feminist theories constitute a revolutionary alternative because they are based on the recognition of the subjective positioning as an analytical starting point, along with all of its variables of gender, class, race, geography and history. This leads to the emergence of knowledge where the consideration of embodied singularity and minoritarian subjectivities become a critical instance against the abstract and fixed museum-like ideas about knowledge. These concepts are rooted within Occidental culture as the products of a universal and disembodied subject. Therefore this counter-narrative privileges women and their cultural and political positioning as the historically minoritarian subjectivities par excellence. In this sense, Adrienne Rich's seminal text "Notes Towards a Politics of Location" (1985) is a fundamental theoretical reference point, speaking against women's oppression. In this text the writer adopts a new discursive practice in direct opposition to the epistemological abstract stance established by the "divine eye" of the white man. Rich, in fact, locates herself as a white, Jewish, North American, middle-class woman. The body in considered with its embodied materiality and its social, cultural, racial, economic and gender differences. From here the body is taken into account as the irreducible premises from which to interrogate us on when, where, how, and in what conditions and relations of power the self demonstrates.

Yet, in the perspective of the politics of location, minoritarian subjectivities are not to be understood as the location of authenticity. The myth of authenticity comes from a process of objectification of the difference between subject and object. This is typical of the politics of identity and the theory of representation, which also concerns artistic productions. Due to this, a counter-narrative of the world based on a combination of feminist precedents and the critical approach of postcolonial studies may offer an attempt to overcome the impasse of objectification by reducing the distance between the object and subject of discourse.

> *Tale, told, to be told . . . / Are you truthful?* Acknowledging the complexities inherent in any speech-act does not necessarily mean taking away or compromising the qualities of a fine story. . . . Who speaks? What speaks? The question is implied and the function named but the individual never reigns, and the subject slips away without naturalising its voice. S/he who speaks, speaks *to* the tale as s/he begins telling and retelling it. S/he does not speak *about* it. For without a certain work of displacement, "speaking about" only partakes in the conservation of systems of binary opposition (subject/object; I/it; We/They) on which territorialized knowledge depends.
>
> (Minh-ha 1992, 327)

Trinh Minh-ha refers to the work of critical displacement and repositioning that is able to undermine the authority of representation and any territorialised knowledge such as that of the nation-state. Here geography turns into a critical field where the concept of space, for example, can be articulated as the negation of the illusion of transparency. The world is constantly embodied. Both discursive and material realities are already continuously connoted by a body in place as well as her differential positioning:

> I am arguing for politics and epistemologies of location, positioning, and situating, where partiality and not universality is the condition of being heard to make rational knowledge claims. These are claims from people's lives; the view from a body, always complex, contradictory, structured and structuring body versus the view from above, from nowhere, from simplicity. . . . Feminism loves another science, the sciences and politics of interpretation, translation, stuttering, and partly understood. Feminism is about the sciences of the multiple subject with (at least) double vision. . . . Feminist embodiment resists fixation and is insatiably curious about the webs of differential positioning.
>
> (Haraway 1991, 193)

Some feminist artists of the 1970s and 1980s, such as Cindy Sherman, Barbara Kruger, Jenny Holzer and Chantal Akermann, explored the relationship between the female body and the (urban) space in critical, investigative and interrogative terms. More recently, this relationship has been further developed and problematised by such transnational artists as Mona Hatoum, Zineb Sedira, Emily Jacir and Lara Baladi, who articulate their experience of migration as a possibility of cultural, geographical and identitarian displacement. In their reconfiguration of the relationship between places, belonging and personal identity, these artists allow for a specific, emblematic expression: autobiography. Here the reflections on limits and differences in addition to the separations and connections between the self and the world are inseparable from the exploration of one's own body:

> What I never quite understood until this writing is that to be without a sex – to be bodiless – as I sought to be to escape the burgeoning sexuality of my adolescence, my confused early days of active heterosexuality, and later my panicked lesbianism, means also to be without a race. I never attributed my removal from physicality to have anything to do with race, only sex, only desire for women.

And yet, as I grew up sexually, it was my race, along with my sex, that was being denied me at every turn.

(Moraga 2000, 125)

In female autobiography, the body emerges as the privileged place for subjective expression since it represents the woman herself, precisely mirroring the neglected and repressed space on which the hegemonic identity of the white man, the autobiographical author par excellence, has been constructed. The result is the universal subject produced by the Western humanist and enlightenment philosophical tradition (Irigaray 2004). Pure *res cogitans*, the subject of Western thought, establishes a precise binary distinction between proper–interior and other–exterior. This subject, a unique and unified centre erected on a stable balance within fixed and impermeable confines, configures himself without his body as pure rational activity. He is abstract matter to which the authority of theorization and the righteousness about the truth of the world is ascribed, owing to his ability to transcend the impure contingencies of human experience to the senses, responsiveness and the body.

The ban of corporality and its instinctual and unruly essence along with the chaotic and grotesque potential it evokes is the founding step of the universal subject. The body is ignored or reduced to a vicarious container of the mind and soul. Knowledge is derived exclusively from a process of dissociation of the self from its physical interdependence with the world. As in the case of Nietzsche's philosophy ([1888]) and Roland Barthes's semiology (1975), even when corporality is recognised as a major player in the formation of personal experience and consciousness, overcoming the mind–body dichotomy, the body is objectified with the attributes specific to the universal subject. Furthermore, in the arguments that position the senses, desires and biology as constitutive elements of the self and conscience, the body is conceived in universalistic terms. As Mikhail Bakhtin put it, it is defined as a "classic body" which is white, male, wealthy, located in the West ([1965]). It represents the naturalized norm to which all the differences of gender, colour, geography, economy, class, ability and even species are perceived as subordinated abnormalities. The objectification of the universal subject's body into normative invisibility does not leave any space for ambiguity, indeterminacy or heterogeneity. It encourages a process of identification according to which those whose bodies diverge from the norm to be paradoxically perceived as essentially bodies and hence singular, irrational, exotic, irregular and unnatural.

The space of the universal subject and that of the culturally grotesque, or socially abject, according to Julia Kristeva, are mutually
constitutive. In her well-known essay on abjection, Kristeva maintains
that social order and "proper" subjectivities, both individual (the universal subject) and collective (the Occidental nation-states) are constructed on the expulsion of the culturally and socially impure and
improper (Kristeva 1982). This is according to a mechanism of abjection immanent in the formation of both subject and sexual categories.
For instance, Judith Butler, recalling Kristeva's observations, shows
how the bolstering of hetero-normativity is based on the rejection or
abjection of homosexuality as a violation of the norm (Butler 1990).
Yet, as Jasbir Puar observes, homosexuality as well (especially male)
has now been rendered normative by today's mainstream nationalist politics of gender equality (above all through the recognition of
same-sex marriages) (Puar 2007). On the one hand, this standardizing
of homosexuality occurs in order to domesticate dissent and create
(new) "docile patriots". On the other hand, queer people, lesbians,
transsexuals and, of course, migrants are what this homonationalism
produces as its constitutive "others". In other words, the consolidation
of the dominant notions of gender and race requires a unification of
difference as abject. Doing so would produce symmetry between the
body as "otherness" and the "others" as abject bodies.

Traditionally, the female body is the abject body par excellence on
which the universal subject monolith is built, on which the borders
between a male exterior and a female interior are inscribed. As Sidonie
Smith observes, "if the topography of the universal subject locates
man's selfhood somewhere between the ears, it locates woman's selfhood between her thighs. The material and symbolic boundary of the
female body becomes the hymen – that physical screen whose presence or absence signals so much" (Smith 1993, 12). In the patriarchal
order, women, exiled from their individuality and from the plurality
of their desires and the legitimacy of their thoughts, are embodied as
"nonreflecting bios" (Smith 1993, 19). They are receptacles of love,
home guardians and caretakers or, alternatively, inhabitants of a (pro-
fessional) space confined to (male) subordination and functionality.
The bodies eliminated by this domesticated vision are those in motion
between multiple identities, cultures, languages and places. They are
lesbian, queer, black, brown, sick, unable, marginal and migrant.
They are the bodies where all these variables can stratify. The hybrid
narratives produced by the migrant and transnational female writers
described by Lidia Curti (2004) are indicative here. Their insubor-
dinate and revolutionary voices constitute an authentic cultural and

political paradigm. If the hegemonic discourse on identity and corporality is built on the exclusion or marginalization of differences, then
the possibility of undoing this mechanism comes from a confrontation
with those very embodied differences. This goes along with a dispo-
sition to encounter the interruptions, voids and discontinuity which
are the indecipherable spaces and blind spots that inevitably negotiate
the alternative perspectives they propose. A shift from disembodied
universal to embodied singularities occurs in autobiographical production. This is understood as a plural way of inscribing the self – *autos*
and *bios*, mind and body, "self" and "other" – by a particular subject
able to decompose the traditional Occidental male canon. This tenet
excluded women because of their particularistic voice[1] opposed to the
laws of conformity, which, as Smith maintains, coordinated and contained "colorfulness".

Differencing the Canon: The Autobiography of Becoming

During the 1970s when feminist theory started to explore the disruptive quality of feminine writing of the self, autobiography became the
privileged means for women within contemporary art. This is due to
it deliberately interrupting the old patriarchal narrative of femininity and the body. As Sidonie Smith and Julia Watson observe, it is
mainly through visual art that women produce counter-narrations
of themselves, as the widely quoted Isak Dinesen's tale, "The Blank
Page" (1957), exemplifies (Smith and Watson 2002; see Gubar 1986).
In a Spanish convent surrounded by linen transplanted from the Holy
Land, nuns spend their time weaving sheets for an aristocratic wed-
ding. Along the corridors the "noble" sheets of the first nuptial night
are exposed, each one marked with the virginal blood, the name of
the bride and the family coat of arms. The exhibition of the bloody
sheets was also a commonly practiced ritual of some Mediterranean
communities, established as a way to certify the bride's "honesty"

---

1 Domna Stanton writes: "the autobiographical, in literary histories, constituted a
  positive term when applied to Augustine, Montaigne, Rousseau and Goethe, Henry
  Adams and Henry Miller, but . . . had negative connotations when imposed on wom-
  en's texts. . . . [The autobiographical] was used to affirm that women could not transcend but only record, the concerns of the private self; thus it has effectively served to
  devalue their writing. . . . wielded as a weapon to denigrate female texts and exclude
  them from the canon" (1984, 132).

and confirm the husband's legitimacy. This is an archive on how the patriarchal values were perpetrated: through penetration, appropriation and "framing" of female sexuality. The traditional Western female autobiography was impressed in the blood and names on the exhibited sheets. Yet, this narrative is interrupted in Dinesen's tale by a blank sheet showing a dissident absence, an insolent refusal of declaration where the possibility of an alternative story uncloses.

Dinesen's tale does not celebrate silence and negation of female virtues. Rather, it casts a shadow of ambiguity on celebrated female candour as it ends up being identified with a gesture of subversion, an interruption of the phallogocentric narrative. The recognisable, marked frame is turned into a blind spot, an indecipherable presence, an unmarked territory. In the words of Peggy Phelan, it corresponds to "a configuration of subjectivity which exceeds, even while informing, both gaze and language" (1993, 27). Beyond the immediately visible, unmarked femininity is evoked here as an interdiction, a dissidence and hence the possibility of different configurations of the subjectivity and body. Significantly, in contemporary arts, the women who are aware of being naturalised by the masculinist logic as the object of the male gaze, or as John Berger observes, "watch[ing] themselves being looked at" (1972, 47), use autobiography in order to deconstruct their objectification by both the artist–producer and the spectator–consumer. Female artists aim at a revaluation of narcissism as a strategic politics of resistance based on a valorisation of the embodied experience and the interconnection between the object and subject of art, the external and internal self: "narcissism, enacted through the body art, turns the subject inexorably and paradoxically outward . . . [it is] a marker of *instability* of both self and other" (Jones 1998, 48).

Female artists reappropriate their bodies and reproduce them in fragments, traces, excesses and remains, evoking the self as an excessive, instable, hybrid, interdependent, collective entity, deconstructing both the artistic canon and identity itself. Female artists show how autobiography is not a neutral and transparent practice mirroring the authenticity of a fixed and sovereign subject. It is inseparable from the immanent and material experience of an embodied subject and her cultural, social, geographical and gender variables. Art historian Griselda Pollock (1999) underlines the need to differentiate the canon, starting from a refusal of the ideal of transparency, which connects an artwork to its author and his life and true intimacy like a codified autobiography. Pollock opposes to the ideal of transparency the difficulty of deciphering or a claim to opacity, which is often inscribed in the female art. Female visual autobiography works within the threshold of different genres and identities, inventing multiple bodies, mask and mixing the techniques into a radical poetic of difference. This difference is female not for the advocacy of an essence but for its rupture of the fixed patriarchal norms of culture, sexuality and identity.

Contemporary feminist autobiographical art radically challenges central power and precept. In doing this it creates counter-discourses based on difference and practices of subjectification and its positioning in the interstices of multiple languages, cultures, geographies and histories. In fact, it is crucial to consider the impact of these minoritarian voices and analyse the relationship between who speaks, who is spoken for, who is spoken to and who listens. The question here concerns representation as a Eurocentric epistemological practice of Occidental philosophical and anthropological tradition. Against representation, female transcultural autobiographies can be considered as a theoretical alternative, which offers new meanings of being-in-the-world.

To rethink subjectivity in terms of embodied singularity implies also a rethinking of the relationship between artistic representation/ exhibition, philosophical and epistemological representation and political and cultural identity in the conceptualization of the "other". The attention on the latter as embodied singularities risks emphasising the (cultural, social, sexual) marginality of lived experience as the site of authenticity. Such (artistic and epistemological) representations could favour an unobserved shift from the ideal of the transparency of knowledge and the unique, unified, fixed self to the ideal of the authenticity of marginal and singular experience, thus getting mixed up in a vain process of metaphorisation, proper to the theory of representation and the politics of identity, based on a crystallisation of differences as representative metaphors of specific identities.

The objectification of identities through a mythologisation of the marginal other as authentic representatives of otherness is, according to Gayatri Chakravorty Spivak (1988), the paradoxical mistake made by poststructuralist critique in its attempts to deconstruct the universal subject and his logocentric vision. Spivak examines the contradictory relationship of the poststructuralist scholars with cultural heterogeneity and marginalisation and denounces the missed consideration of the power relationship between themselves and those who they consider as marginal others. This asymmetrical and neglected relation of power between the subjects and the objects of a discipline "restores the category of the sovereign subject within the theory that seems most to question it" (Spivak 1999, 261). As Spivak stresses, it perpetuates the hegemonic epistemological approach of the Western tradition of speaking for, concealing or overshadowing the different power relations between the subject and the object of discourse. Thus, in the discourse of these privileged "hegemonic radicals", the non-Western natives, for example, are excluded from any production of theoretical discourse or historical meaning and are relegated to a subordinate position. This position is necessary to the functioning of a Eurocentric representation of a white consciousness; the same position Immanuel Kant assigned them three centuries ago, representing the limit-case of reason or, as Mbembe has recently argued (2017), even the non-existence and illegitimacy of such an idea as a black reason. For instance, as bell hooks observed, "racism is perpetuated when blackness is associated solely with concrete, gut-level experience, conceived as either opposing or having no connection to abstract thinking and the production of critical theory" (hooks 1990, 23). Even a radical discourse like post-structuralism can bring with it the germs of exoticism and racism when the power relations are not considered. Otherness and marginality end up being essentialised as authentic and anti-universalistic. Essentialism is an instrumental fiction that, as hooks underlines, avoids taking into account the impact of globalisation and postmodernism on the so-called non-Western marginal others.

Similarly, even some parts of feminist art and critique show how the risk of essentialism is always around the corner. If the feminist position shares postcolonial theory with postmodern aesthetics, the sustainability of a decentred, plural and becoming subject and a dismantling of the universalistic norm and authority, it takes distance from them, as Griselda Pollock maintains (1999), when it claims a biological female essence for this subjectivity. On the contrary, far from considering "Third World" women as privileged signifiers of difference (postmodern automatons), Rey Chow proposes studying the various strategies of coalition between feminism and postmodernism, and above all between feminism and postcoloniality (Chow 1992). She defines this interstitial space of alternative possibilities as "critical regionalism", where the complexity of the local assumes particular relevance.

It is possible to conceive and produce a different kind of representation of the self with an approach to the world and the self in relational, dynamic, creative terms, rather than in prescriptive or oppositive ones. Assia Djebar's writings, where she mingles autobiography, history and fiction, indicate the possibility of emancipating representation from its colonial look. In the foreword to her book, *Women of Algiers in Their Apartment* ([1980]), for instance, she is very careful to make it clear that she does not "speak for" Arab women: "not to aim to speak for or, still worse, to 'speak about', hardly even to speak *close to*, and if possible *right up against*: that is the first of the solidarities to assume towards the few Arabic women who obtain or acquire freedom of movement, both of body and of spirit" (Djebar [1980], 8). Djebar's claim to speak close to or right up against implies an epistemological and cultural turn in our approach to the world and its many different subaltern subjectivities. In this way, alternative narratives could also be created to align adequately with the contemporary planetary and diasporic configuration of the world and the mobile constellation of multiple belongings.

Contemporary autobiographies by female artists offer another theoretical tool, insisting on the embodied experience of subjectivities that are simultaneously decentred, fragmented, mobile, becoming and irreducibly immanent. The capacity of these artists to configure themselves as both subject and object of representation does not imply the claiming of an agency of female subjectivity per se, as Rosalind Krauss maintains (1999). It produces a break in the obstinacy of genre and the positions of spectators, destabilizing the process of identification.

It is in the encounter with the other that recalls and interrogates the other within the self that a new theoretical and aesthetic sense of autobiography can be produced. In her autobiography, *What Does a Woman Want? Reading and Sexual Difference*, Shoshana Felman questions the premises on which theories on feminist art are based, and advocates an inversion. Instead of thinking of women as the subjects par excellence of opposition and resistance, the writer suggests "feminine resistance of the text" (Felman 1993, 133), that is, reading within the texts signs of resistance to the patriarchal assumptions and dominant paradigms, thus indicating the way toward a becoming feminist. Felman's proposal recognises the necessity of questioning even one's own personal assumptions. Feminism gives to the personal a crucial importance, rendering women's experiences as a counter-measure to official knowledge. The personal, Felman observes, is a rather problematic alternative, as it is not a guarantee. Women cannot always trust their self, as this is always a cultural external construction, without a proper and singular autobiography. She writes:

> I will suggest that *none of us, as women, has as yet, precisely, an autobiography*. Trained to see ourselves as objects and to be positioned as the Other estranged to ourselves, we have a story that cannot by definition be self-present to us, a story that, in other words, is not a story, but *must become* a story. . . . And it cannot become a story except through the *bond of reading*, that is, through the *story of the Other* (the story read by other women, the story told by other women, the story of women told by others)

insofar as this story of the other , as our own autobiography, *has yet precisely to be owned*. . . . I will propose that we might be able to engender, or to access our story only indirectly – by conjugating literature, theory, and autobiography together through the act of reading and by reading, thus, into the texts of culture, at once our sexual difference and our autobiography as missing.

(Felman 1993, 14)

The sense of one's own autobiography lies in a critical connectivity and in the possibility of implementing multiple belongings. It lies in the vision of the self as a point of interferences, processes, transits and mobilities that are defined by the practice of relation and the politics of location. The ideology of the same, the centre and the authority, as well as of the self as a stable, indisputable essence, can be overcome in an autobiographical practice where a reflection on the self is inseparable from an act of projection from oneself. The encounter with differences moves beyond the monologue of the self with the self, taking it into a more fragile and challenging region.

The Poetics of Collage and the Art of Relations

The discussion about contemporary geography within the critical framework of visual culture; the cultural and political forms of obsession and resistance to borders; the philosophical and cultural question of Occidental, universalistic representation and identity; and female autobiographical expressions as critical and alternative narrations of the self and the world converge now into an analysis of what is defined here as the "poetics of collage". This refers to the collage aesthetics and technique produced by transcultural artists seen as forms of epistemological, cultural, historical and political critique against the (Western, white and masculinist) rhetoric of identity and nationalism as well as the cultural and social "norms" of recognition and abjection that sustain them.

A brief contextualisation of collage may be useful here. In Europe, in the period between colonisation and the First World War, such artists as Braque and Picasso introduced the collage technique. This technique unfolded audacious and stimulating possibilities for artistic expression and was a substantial innovation in the process of painting and its materiality. European and US artists did not limit themselves to the use of colour as an artistic means, but they drew from the most diverse sources: pieces of newspaper, textiles, photographs, paper, plastic, wood. They pushed formal research beyond the traditional technology of colour and paintbrush, giving residence on the frame to heterogeneous daily matter. In the creative detachment from the fundamental and unquestioned instruments of traditional painting, artists gave an aesthetic and expressive value to a practice that was focused on the most immediate ordinary reality, on ordinary materiality. They then gathered, recollected, assembled and pasted. Thus making art correspond to a kind of sartorial and ecological activity, which was also prosaic and ludic, of recycling and montage, and hence, an attempt to recuperate and recreate a reality broken into pieces and fragments, fallen apart under the blows of historical violence.

In some ways collage announced a distance and dislocation of the transcendental modes of thought, observation and action, based on a cultural attitude prone to legitimate monolithic ideas of unity, supremacy, power and authenticity. In fact, the collage technique revolves around a decentring of the artistic transcendent and calls into question the very possibility of a cultural decentring. This subsequently favoured immediacy and marginality, humble daily life and existence, what is usually taken aside and hidden in the invisible zones of the taken-for-granted. The modernist collage, as well as Duchamp's ready-made, the kitsch aesthetic of pop art and its attention to common and commoditized products, announced emancipation from the previous ways of perceiving and understanding reality. Yet it was an emancipation that was nonetheless circumscribed by the limits of Eurocentrism, Occidentalism and patriarchy. This is also what happens with postmodern devices of pastiche or palimpsest, where aesthetic language plays with mixture, confusion, alteration and juxtaposition yet rarely gains the dimension of a radical political questioning. Generally, it appears formally and culturally complex without being simultaneously politically subversive. Therefore the displacement and questioning of the cultural transcendent unhinged by those practices privilege the recognition of a "close" marginality, without recognizing its capacity to question the geographical, historical and cultural frames where it developed. Art opens up to the marginal, avoiding the danger of scrutinizing and challenging its own dominant position.

A different example is given by the self-portrait, which uses collage as an instrument of critical evolution. The self-portrait is a deeply political, autobiographical statement, even able to appropriate and deconstruct, affirm and subvert actual epistemological codes. Since the 1920s, and more incisively during the 1970s, such artists as Hanna Hoch, Claude Cahun, Louise Bourgeois, Nancy Spero, Miriam Shapiro and Carol Rama have used collage and weaving (Parker 2010) in the articulation of their aesthetics, aiming at a valuation of their marginal position as transcultural female artists. These artists, spanning the first- and second-wave feminist art generations, show their enduring ability to fragment and reconstruct the subject. It is possible to perceive in the collage's subversive stiches a new cultural and political mode of understanding the self, as an attack on and detachment from the Occidental masculinist normativity. Each artist adopts collage as a radical word, embracing collision and weaving and an affective spectrum running from the slow pulse of stitch and weave to sharp, kinetic shock. Each considers images of or about women as a "body politic", a site of resistance. Catherine de Zegher, for instance, observes:

> In these works, aesthetic negotiation of the subject mirrors back to the viewer an imaginary bodily unity – as other and as cultural other – exposed, shattered, and collaged in pieces reiterating a fantasy of a chaotic body, fluid and fragmentary . . . mocking the ideal of plenitude, with its illusion of homogenization (difference subsumed by wholeness), these works criticized political issues of representation of race, class, and gender.
>
> (de Zegher 1996, 25)

Transcultural feminist aesthetics extend the critique against the reason of the strongest, insisting on claiming forms of existence that are coalitions, affiliations or constellations of belongings and disjunctions. One of the several crucial elements that can be envisaged in the new forms of signification linked to this aesthetic theory and practice is the historical decline of the idea of an individualized subject produced by the Occidental phallogocentric order. There is also the research of new forms of subjectivities, new modes of being in the world, in opposition to what Caren Kaplan and Inderpal Grewal defined as "scattered hegemonies" (1994): the diverse forms of patriarchal collusion proliferated all around the world. Looking at the complexity of postmodernity, the authors reflect on the necessity of considering feminist practices within globalised dynamics of transnational cultural and economic fluxes as well as of the counter-measures of ethnic and racial nationalisms and fundamentalisms. The authors, thus, see in feminist practices the possibility of cutting across and overcoming the universalizing tendencies of both the modernist centred subject and the decentred subject of postmodernity.

Chow, for instance, proposes exploring the diverse forms of affiliations between women in different communities, showing how "the careful rejection of postmodernist abandon as a universalist politics goes hand in hand with its insistence on the need to *detail history*, in the sense of cutting it up so that as it gains more ground in the social struggle, sexual difference becomes a way of engaging not simply with women but with other types of subjugation" (1992, 115). Then, she closes with Elisabeth Weed's words: "if sexual difference becomes ever more destabilized, living as a female will become an easier project, but that will result from the continued displacement of 'women', not from its consolidation" (Chow 1992, 115). In regards to contemporary artistic practices this discourse translates into a poetics of collage that register women's insistence on multiple differences, where sex, gender, class and race intersect and a narration of history in details, fragments and at the same time connections, points of suture with other histories and otherness. This poetics of collage creates critical zones of contacts between racially, socially, economically and/or sexually oppressed subjects, but it can also concerns new frontiers in the imaginary of hybrid belongings. As Donna Haraway recommends in her latest book (2016), in a damaged and unhealthy world, totally colonised by man and capital, the only way we can survive is to construct non-genealogical communities and relationships with non-human beings, in a now obliged symbiosis with the "others" of any species (mineral, vegetal, animal, technological).

Collage's dynamic, chimerical logic of fragmentation and suture continues to open new angles on sexual, postcolonial and cultural identities, playing on the border between self and other, fact and fiction, here and elsewhere, past and future, violence and desire. Australian artist Paula do Prado uses collage to probe racial, gender and cultural stereotypes. She questions identity and authenticity, remixing and reframing in her own self-portraits such female figures as the "mulatta" or "jezebel" drawn from her Afro-Uruguayan heritage and the odalisque as idealised non-white women. Similarly, in her collages the Kenyan- and New York-based artist Wangechi Mutu questions the way women are represented in Western culture and disrupts common stereotypes by introducing animal and machine parts into her images, thus unfolding a disrupting queer imaginary drawn from femininity. The now famous black cut-out silhouettes by African American artist Kara Walker explore questions of gender and race, examining the atrocities of the past and the on-going tensions that still exist in the United States today. Often underscored by a dark humour and infused with a Goya-esque nightmarish quality, Walker's silhouettes subvert historical stereotypes about African Americans and a traditional romanticised vision of American past by overlapping provocatively extreme acts of violence and acts of sexual explicitness. Walker also uses traditional collaging methods, mixing texts and images. In these unsettling explorations of the American history of racism and its confluence of disgust and desire, black females play a crucial role. In her collages, the Turkish artist Canan Senol addresses the oppression and harassment of women by family, government and religion through a mixture of the old and the new, tradition and modernity, deconstructing the supremacy of the male gaze over the female body. Egyptian artist Ghada Amer, who is more frequently associated with drawing and painting, also uses collage to challenge religion and patriarchy by claiming the senses and the body through ambiguous and distorted images of female sexual pleasure, which are simultaneously veiled and explicit, hidden and shown, seducing and scandalous. Many other artists use collage, paying tribute to a female and feminist art historical lineage, contributing to the construction of a transcultural critical region of both cultural dissent and alternative. In this book analysis is focused on the digital collages produced by the Egyptian–Lebanese artist Lara Baladi, considered in terms of autobiographical "critical regions" composed of heterogeneous images coming from the constellation of the artist's multiple belongings. In Baladi's nomadic and heterotopic aesthetics, the use of collage meets a need to evoke the geographical and cultural multiplicity of the artist's world and experiences, conflating fiction and reality, myth, fairy tales and dreams. Baladi's collages involve an infinite collection of voices, places, tongues, stories, events and subjects. These elements interlace and participate with one another, creating a world of reversibility and upset, conjunctions and disjunctions, multi-layering and dilation. The artist creates critical regions, sewed with "subversive stiches", in counterpoint to permanence, fixity and immobility.

The expression and narration of the self, embodiment and carnal aesthetic of female postcolonial art can be considered as the site where border art and border thought meet and interlace, displacing the cultural, geographical, historical, social and sexual confines of the self. In this movement between cultures and identities, a chance is offered to create new coalitions, alliances and relations across and against the hegemonic definitions and institutions of community, common life and sense.

2 Narrations
Transcultural Memories and Migrations

Postcolonial Art and the World Museum

The museum, the institution of memory, is historically the place where identity is constructed. It was born in the West, precisely to generate national identity, to produce a knowledge of one's own culture, and simultaneously an ability to overwhelm the other's culture. A harmonious alliance of three fundamental activities guarantees its existence: possession, conservation and exhibition. Traditionally, the museum is considered the place of collection, where, as Mieke Bal observes, "preservation is the precondition of exhibition, as well as property is the precondition for conservation" (1996, 65), according to a system of subsistence similar and intimately linked to the nation. In the museums of collection the exhibited object has a holy aura, both as a "domestic product" and a gained good, and it is preserved through a careful activity of storage. For instance, as Remo Bodei observes, "museums represent a kind of big *templar* enclosure (*templum* has the Greek root *temno*, which means to cut, to separate) or a frame that, as in a picture, separates the aesthetic area from the unaesthetic one" (2004, 164), yet one whose symbolic and immaterial power invests both with a nationalistic yield. What is exposed to the public admiration is what the nation has been able to produce and win in terms of art, culture, technology and science. The function of the museum is based on a capitalist system aimed at profit, above all symbolic, related to the nation's growth, power and superiority. In this sense, the exhibiting function can be considered the ultimate stage of the nation's colonialist mechanism of cultural reproduction, resulting from the public fruition of the conquered, accumulated, preserved and exhibited objects. But, inexorably, the nation-museum is counted among the "victims" of the centrifugal currents generated by advanced globalisation. The self-referential dream of conservation is destined to fade away, under the global backlash.

The museum, as a nationalist enclave, is overwhelmed by different fluxes between nations, which Arjun Appadurai defines as the "diasporic, public sphere" (1996, 36). Thus it loses credibility as the exclusive cultural reference frame of a nation.[1] In the global era, the museum stops being a reserve, a place of confinement, or a "heterotopia", as Michel Foucault would say ([1967]): a place where the visitor is isolated from the outer world and its movements, finding himself imprisoned into an obsolete space-time category, in a naive, anachronistic or, even worse, nostalgic, chronotopia. Compared to the kind of openness the current times now require, the museum, in its traditional form and meaning, can only be considered a tomb, a mausoleum, a mo(nu)ment of the past, re-collecting the ruins of itself and the nation. Here, the remains, the rest of, or, I would say, the limits of an entire culture are laid bare.

It seems that the museum – as the institution of national tradition, memory and identity – shares with the nation a similar inexorable destiny of physical and ideological decline, which has lasted for many years now, as a consequence of the diverse processes of migration activated by the global economic system. In fact, the museum institution acknowledges its own precariousness and transforms itself. It is a process inaugurated above all by contemporary art, with its accentuated mobility, hybridity and lack of a definite centrality, as both a product and a producing agent of the modern deterritorialization to which Appadurai refers (1996).

The museum, in the European context, underwent the erosive action of art, beginning with the avant-garde period in the early twentieth century and continuing with the artistic movements of the 1960s and 1970s. In these periods, through its protesting flow against political power and bourgeois conformism, art aroused debate, controversy and even violent reactions from both specialists and the public, precisely because it announced something that diverged from common sense and sensibility, consolidated styles and official contexts.[2] The

---

1 According to Appadurai's well-known thesis, postmodernity is characterised by a diffused and disarticulated deterritorialisation of people, images, technologies, capitals and ideas – which he defines respectively as "ethnoscapes", "mediascapes", "technoscapes", "financescapes" and "ideoscapes" – which jeopardise any form of cultural unity, presumably homogeneous and closed within spatially defined borders such as the nation-state (1996).

2 In particular, I am referring to the Dada movement with its emphasis on the identification of art and life, collective creation, public implication, hazard, desecration, parody, paradox and critical creativity. I also refer to other movements, from situationism to Fluxus, which have returned to, rethought and developed these themes.

implication for political and social dimensions, the protest against the institutional places and manifestations, with the subsequent questioning of their legitimacy and function, encouraged the museums to open themselves toward artistic research. It was, however, primarily the configuration of art as a relational experience (Bourriaud [1998]) that was developed in the latter decades – with its emphasis on ethical responsibility, interactive opportunities and the move from canonical places, such as museums, to the outer territory (Hooper-Greenhill 2000). In this sense, a creative confrontation with space was established (as the experiences of "public art" and "environmental art" testify), and new subjectivities were produced which transformed the nature of the place for art, as well as the artistic object itself.

This kind of art lives outside the traditional places of art. It is itself able to create new relational spaces, enabling states of encounter, modalities of conviviality and social participation, where the interaction with the public is a substantial part of the artwork. Here "making art", the "art working" or the aesth-et(h)ics acquires a social dimension and value (Ettinger 2006). This is a kind of art which involves, as Stuart Hall (2001) maintains, a transformation of the museum into a "post-museum" – that is a relativisation of the museum, no longer perceived as the exclusive place for art, but just one of the many places where aesthetic practices circulate (even though the museum's role in the production and reproduction of cultural capital still keeps its traditional power and prestige).

Yet what can decisively contribute to the transformation of the museum that is already in place is the postcolonial art produced by migrant subjects, mainly coming from the Western empire's former colonies. This kind of "migrant art" produces a "migrant" and "postcolonial" sense of the world: an anti-nationalist, non-exclusive, non-possessive, non-binary and not rigidly defined sense of the world. The aesthetic of such artists as Mona Hatoum, Zineb Sedira and Lara Baladi powerfully displays the sense of an alternative reality. A dispersed, fluctuating, "uprooted" geography defines these artists' identity and insistently informs their art. The places they create evoke the heterogeneous, differential, vertiginously contradictory nature of being "in-between": between different histories, between different cultures, between different tongues, between different memories, showing how, beyond its traumas, the experience of migration inscribes border-crossings and engenders new relations along them. As Édouard Glissant puts it, "a tale of errancy is a tale of relation" ([1990], 143): a tale speaking about dislocation as well as relocation. The artists are in a certain sense able to reterritorialise themselves, yet they are irreducible to any instance of rootedness. Their aesthetics draw a personal territoriality made of the traces, the residues, the remains that their crossings have left behind, showing a life path beyond the borders of nationality and its delimiting identifications.

The precariousness of the self, displayed in this aesthetics of the inappropriable, directly questions the nation and its narration of the world according to pretextual, if not opportunist, divisions between citizens and migrants, North and South, West and East. It also questions the place and time of subjectivity and those of art itself. Can the museum be a proper place for art? Can the contemporary be the exclusive time for art? Emancipated from its classic function of preserving, archiving, collecting and exhibiting – as well as from the current function of museums of contemporary art of artistic certification and global tourism, as happens with "museum brands" such as the Guggenheim – the museum can be considered an open space for wandering: the site of a living memory, of narration, of conversation, of migration. This recalls the need, as Iain Chambers suggests, "to reconfigure museology on a map exceeding the requirements imposed by a national, almost exclusively Western, point of view" (Rivera Magos 2009). The museum needs to give an account of historical movements and itself become movement and a place where the democracy of European or national identity and memory can be negotiated. As Viv Golding suggests, it is possible to see in new poetic practices a creative way to bring the museum out of the bottlenecks of authoritarian culture and patriarchy, thus liberating the world's creolised voices and visions:

> To begin to break down the patriarchal barriers of power and control that traditionally characterise museums . . . the possibility of the museum as a site to forge fresh alliances, where creative people might help visitors' imaginings of new relationships. I contend that it is primarily creolised voices that inspire innovative forms of expression, impelling movement beyond the master's language . . . active possibilities for museums to address inequalities in global capitalist economies, by providing creative pathways – poetics to raise new voices and visibilities in the museum and more critical thinking in the wider world.
>
> (Golding 2013, 81–2)

Here a dynamic and contemporary sense of memory emerges. A memory of specific places and times exists, and it still needs to be recognized and respected, not for what is circumscribed and fixed in its own specificity, but for what is considered in the possibility of connection with other places and other times. This means considering memory in its trans-historicity, as a necessity which the processes and experiences of migration recall.

For example, Homi Bhabha, analysing the work of the poet and critic Adrienne Rich, speaks about a trans-historical memory enabling an ethical and affective identification with globality (Bhabha 1996). Aware of the traumatic effect of brutal events such as war, the Holocaust, slavery or displacing personal experiences such as migration and exile, Rich describes a type of counter-memory of places and times which takes into account the singularity of each historical event. Through the poetic instrument of memory, Rich's contributions create a profound sense of respect, identification, compassion and responsibility and hence a broader and shared sense of community. According to Bhabha, the value of Rich's work does not consist so much in her ability to highlight a historical and cultural connection between different places and times but rather in the necessity, in light of that connection, to revisit and rethink what was considered one's own history, giving an account of it in critical terms. In this way, the historical conscience can become a fundamental factor of connection between the subjects that are able to share it and configure it as a form of intervention or collective participation in contemporary reality which asks us to confront our condition of proximity as inhabitants of transnational spaces. For Bhabha, contemporaneity is a "translational space" (1996, 201): a hybrid space, a space of transit and resistance, an interstitial temporality. In this space the return to an essentialist identitarian conscience cohabits with a tendency to a constant process of fragmentation and transformation in a state of flowing interpenetration of the specific and the common, the local and the global.

Bhabha's analysis of the use of memory in Rich's work as a critical instrument for the achievement of a common historical conscience and the difficult negotiation between local and global can also be extended to Hatoum, Sedira and Baladi's art of memory and the way it invests and overcomes the "museum". The latter, if it is understood classically as the place for the preservation of national memory or in its modern configuration as a place of cultural hyper-consumption, can now be articulated as a space for historical storytelling: the place of narrative memory, of unlimited connection and sharing, of trespassing the physical borders of the location where the tale had taken place. The artworks of these migrant artists are able to give a dialogic and evocating value to the exhibiting space they inhabit, weaving bonds with the territorial reality and also between the territorial and global reality. The museum becomes the space where it is possible to intercept, within locality, the traces of globality, and hence to recognize and negotiate the threads woven between close and distant stories, past and present, here and elsewhere, and between common and personal memory (Ferrara 2012; Chambers 2012).

A possibility opens up here, of applying the Gramscian invitation to "think globally" (Gramsci [1948–51]) to the field of museology, to try to emancipate it from provincialism and nationalism. This would mean extending one's thought in a global sense, making one's thought global rather than colonial, which only leads to further confinement. Instead, the Gramscian turn in one's thinking should be processed in a postcolonial sense, that is by trying to stretch one's vision of the world beyond the limits of the "proper" (understood both as material and immaterial patrimony), until one welcomes the eventuality of its radical questioning. It would involve transforming the traditional paradigm of the "museum-nation" into the postcolonial one of a "museum-world", namely a "becoming-migrant" of the museum, as it is precisely in this particular "becoming-minoritarian" that the museum can be defined as global.

Lampedusa: A Living Archive of Modernity

Migration is not simply a social problem, an economic phenomenon, and an individual tragedy; rather, it can be traced back to the age of the colonial conquests of overseas territories by European countries and the subsequent formation of the global trade – from the forced transportation of enslaved Africans to the Americas, to the present movement from the south of the world. How we understand migration clearly has an impact upon the understanding of Occidental modernity, its institutional organization, and national(ist) narration of memory, which is confined to fixed historiographical sequences of past and present (Chambers 2008). Our world, therefore, can be understood in terms of an interlacing of histories and a concatenation of distinct worlds, as Achille Mbembe put it, where colonialism is an open-ended process that has a crucial role for the circulation of goods, human beings, and collective imaginaries: "From every point of view, the 'plantation', the 'factory' and the 'colony' were the principal laboratories in which experiments were conducted into the authoritarian destiny of the world that we see today" (Mbembe 2008).

Mediterranean migrations could be regarded as an integral part of an extensive transnational history driven by a planetary political economy that constantly reiterates a logic of accumulation and exploitation. The liberal fiction of "intercultural dialogue" often negates the injustice of asymmetrical relationships of power together with the unequal distribution of economic and cultural capital that has shaped the planetary formation of the modern world. This is a well-known and highly debated story, yet how much of this complex issue comes to be registered and acknowledged seems to be an irresolvable question. Who, in the present political economy of the world, has the power to speak? This immediately recalls the famous and still open question posed by Gayatri Spivak in her influential essay "Can the Subaltern Speak?" (1988) about three decades ago, where she highlights not so much the silence of subalterns (Hindu women, in that case) or their inability to speak, but rather an incapability, or even an unwillingness, to listen to their voices.

Thinking of and practising new paradigms of narrating history seems to be a cultural challenge for archiving and museum institutions and their nationalist narration of memory. An example may be represented by the possessions of migrants exhibited in Lampedusa, in the summer of 2013, which are part of a wider project about archiving and narrating migration, the Museum of Migrations in Lampedusa, founded by the Askavusa collective and the musician and artist Giacomo Sferlazzo (see Fig. 2.1). The temporary exhibition, entitled "With the Objects of the Migrants" included objects found in the boats used by "clandestine" migrants to cross the Mediterranean and then abandoned at the island's public dump, now known as the "cemetery of the boats" (Fig. 2.2). Each object was part of the remains of a shipwreck; each of them was a material and, at the same time, a narrative reminder of transit, migration and survival. Each object was a ruin. There were objects of repair and refreshment, such as a packet of couscous, a rusting teapot, a life jacket, blankets and medicines, the Koran and the Bible, along with personal objects like plastic sandals, toothbrushes and ruined photographs, all displayed neatly on a wooden platform in the middle of the room. On the opposite wall, worn pages of handwritten diaries or letters were exhibited in glass cases, thus generating a direct dialogue with the objects below, along with a dilated sense of the island, both geographically and historically. In fact, the languages of those writings, from Arabic to Bengali, testify to the varied belonging of the migrants and the global routes of contemporary Mediterranean crossings.

In the exhibition, mundane objects, washed ashore or abandoned, acquired a new meaning once they had been displaced from anonymous lives to the exhibitionary logic of the display case. What persists in these salvaged objects is the violent interval or suspension that marks their passage from everyday life (and death) to this quayside

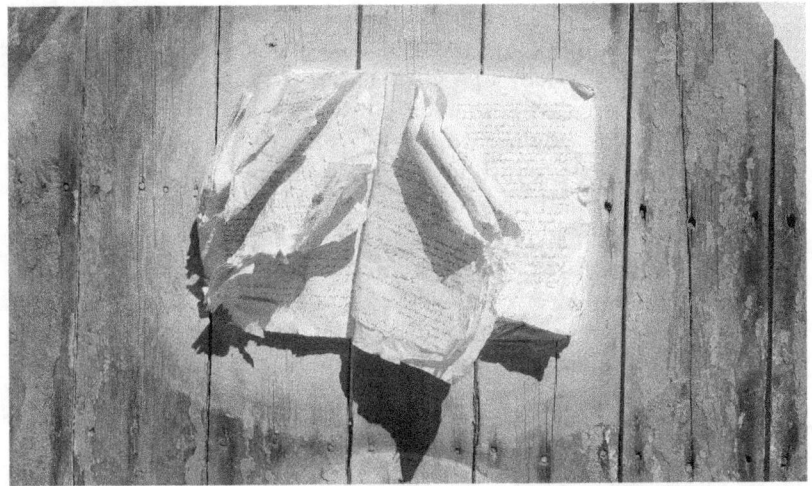

Figure 2.1 Giacomo Sferlazzo, *Nell'aria, nella terra e nel mare* (detail). Piece of boat, sacred text and oil paint, 2010.

© Giacomo Sferlazzo. Courtesy of the artist

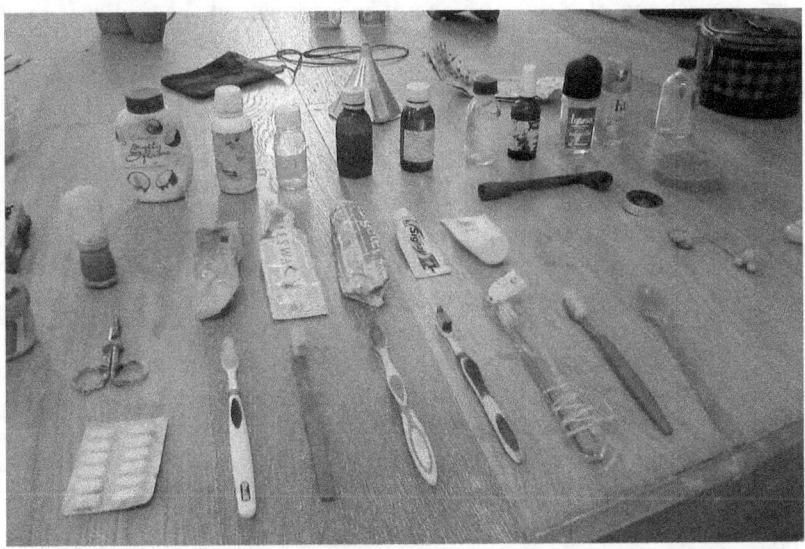

Figure 2.2 "With the Objects of the Migrants". Exhibition at Area Marina Protetta, Lampedusa, 2013.

Photo: Celeste Ianniciello

building in the port of Lampedusa. On the edges, and beyond the boundaries of institutional legitimacy and its representation, the temporary exhibition housed on this dusty island in the seas of Tunisia refuses to lend itself easily to the fetishisation of art. On the contrary, it is a sample of an artistic orientation towards participation and collaboration that has grown exponentially since the early 1990s and has been described by Claire Bishop as "participatory art" in which people constitute the central artistic medium (2012). Indeed, this exhibition propels us into a global phenomenon, where the work of art as a finite item is reconsidered as a long-term and open-ended project, and the spectators are not conceived as viewers, but rather as participants who actively produce and share meanings.

Similarly, as James Clifford crudely pointed out in his recent talk at the Collecting Geographies: Global Programming and Museums of Modern Art conference at the Stedelijk Museum in March 2014, museums could stop being fixed on distanced objects and instead focus more consistently on the stories, the bodies and the cultural crossings associated with those objects. In other words, this would implicate a crucial and critical passage from objects to processes. The key point is to emphasise the collective political horizon inscribed in artistic activities, such as the exhibition in Lampedusa, where interdisciplinary research, an affective and aware engagement of the audience and an experimental curatorial practice are mutually related.

The innovative experience of the Museum of Migrations in Lampedusa, after underhand attempts at appropriation by different government and museum institutions, has been transformed into a new archiving and narrative project: *Porto M: Practices of Memory, Politics and Community*. This was created through the initiative of Askavusa collective, and marked by anti-institutional and independent instances. Here the space and time of narration are left only to the objects and their interrogative and affective presence, and hence the chance to "find the way that brought us to that dump" (Collettivo Askavusa n.d.). Refusing the museum logic of plenitude and objectifying preservation and subverting the humanitarian stereotypes of clandestinity, fragility, need and violence produced by the dominant representations of migration, *Porto M* transforms the migrants' possessions into producers of memory and new cultural meanings which invest the traditional sense of community and recall the traces of a different humanity. The materials of human waste become pieces of art and memory that come to disturb and contest our nationalist ideas of being the legitimate and exclusive inhabitants of Europe. In this post-museum space, which promotes critical strategies of memorialisation, overcoming the "exhibitionary complex" (Bennett 1988) as an end in itself, spectators are transposed with their sensorial bodies into a porous political space, a "contact zone" between citizens and stories (Pratt 1991). Here the "First World" is called to interrogate itself rather than the "other". In this sense we are reminded of the fact that, as Iain Chambers observes, "the precariousness of the migrant is also ours" and that we share with her an "uprooted geography" (2008, 17). The unexpected, the inhospitable, the unarchivable come and contaminate "our history", the linear narration through which our sense of belonging, heritage and the borders of citizenship have been constructed. *Porto M*, as well as Lampedusa itself, can be considered as the space of a trans-historical memory, in the sense indicated by Homi Bhabha, or as a contact zone between past and present, as a fluid archive of a migrant modernity.

From a disciplining, conservator and boundary device, the museum is thus transformed into an unstable entity, exceeding its white walls (Curti 2012) and opening itself to the possibility of a "postcolonial museum" (Chambers et al. 2014) that can rewrite the European legacy, starting from the irrepressible presence of subaltern voices and stories as the tangible traces of a colonial past still rarely recognised. The curatorial, artistic and archiving experiment of *Porto M* and the postcolonial aesthetics developed around experiences of migration bring a cut, an interruption inside the institutional borders of museum knowledge and power, transforming the archive from dead matter to living question. Cultural memory is made elastic and permeable, recalled to other postcolonial places and times, interlacing proximity and distance, past and present, thus indicating the possibility of understanding the Mediterranean in terms of complexity and variability within a critical emerging connection (Hordern et al. 2006). Contemporary art, through experimental participative, affective, autobiographical, political, post-representative practices, reveals an ability to break into history and interrupts the exclusivist and totalising maps of the world, transposing us into the living archive of modernity.

The Fluid (Auto)biography of Zineb Sedira

The autobiographical aesthetics of the French–Algerian artist Zineb Sedira can be defined as Mediterranean with an expression evoking the artist's multiple (Algerian, French, English) geographical, cultural and historical belongings. This multiplicity is inscribed into the hybrid and indefinite images of the artist, of her family and their inhabited or crossed territories, recalling an autobiographical theory and practice that are on the border of the self, between the inside and the outside, the familiar and the strange, the North and the South, in a "third", porous, diasporic space of identity and belonging, which rewrites a fluid cartography. Through an aesthetic of opacity, Sedira highlights the complexity of her intercultural identity, thus interrupting, eroding, and undoing the cultural borders of nationalism, monolingualism, and the geographical borders established by the neo-liberal transnationalism. Sedira's art evokes Ranjana Khanna's idea of a "cut into the force-fields", that is, a critical intervention that questions the material structures and cultural superstructures concerning identity, protection and control, constructed by a "virile community" (Khanna 2008).

In her first artistic production, Sedira focused on the importance of claiming a female cultural genealogy, recognising a feminine subversive power that contrasts the masculinist power of subordination and stereotyping rooted in patriarchal culture and society. The artist lingered on the pain of separation from the motherland and on the generational conflicts linked to the experience of migration, but she also exalted the transformative possibilities inscribed in that experience and the passage through different languages, cultural landscapes. Sedira catches the opportunity to construct new visions – fluid, ambiguous, free imaginaries – from the diverse Mediterranean interlacements of her biographical paths. Born in Paris from Algerian parents who had migrated to France because of the economical difficulties generated by the Algerian war of independence, she grew up in the Parisian *banlieux*, then moved to London where she studied at the Slade School of Arts. Sedira started her career with a series of works where her English formation mingled with her French experience and Algerian heritage and influences, recombining the transcultural context that marks her biography. Lindsey Moore, for example, observes how Sedira's art is more concerned with the sense of multiple cultural and geographical overlapping than with images of definite contexts (Moore 2008). Sedira's could be defined as "the secret art of invisibility", an expression used by Homi Bhabha to describe the art of postcolonial migrant poets (Bhabha 1994). The latter, he explains, question the space of representation and challenge the too clearly defined borders of otherness, breaking the illusion of the stability of the self based on the correspondence between image and identity. The invisibility consists of the ambivalence inscribed in the postcolonial subject's history of mobility, and it constitutes a powerful means of resistance for the migrant woman to the dangers of stereotyping, racism and oppression: "the migrant woman can subvert the perverse satisfaction of the racist, masculinist gaze that disavows her presence, by presenting it with an anxious absence, a counter-gaze that turns the discriminatory look, which denies her cultural and sexual difference, back on itself" (Bhabha 1994, 67).

The reference to a culturally indeterminate perception of identity is evident in the visual triptych *Self Portraits or the Virgin Mary* (2000), where the artist draws herself wholly enveloped in her mother's *haïk*, in the total white of an immaculate vision, like the Christian Virgin Mary, yet contaminated by the Islamic "Algerian white" (Djebar [1996]). Here the cultural and visual ambiguity produces a constant oscillation between doubt and certainty, so that, as Joseph McGonagle observes, "the images may seem at first more about self-effacement than self-portraiture" (2007, 220). Through what can be considered as an exercise in subversion and disorientation, the artist recalls the interlacing of Christianity and Islam, different Mediterranean cultures and traditions, beyond national borders and their monolithic representations.

In her video-installation *Mother Tongue* Sedira addresses again questions of cultural opacity and plurality. The work presents three screens where the artist herself appears first with her child, then with her mother, and then just her mother and her child on the third screen. A conversation is in progress between them about childhood memories: Sedira's mother speaks Arabic, her daughter English and the artist French, owing to the different geographies where their personal stories took place. But the different languages used to reconstruct their memories does not allow a mutual understanding, and the dialogue is fragmented in different yet interlaced monologues. A transnational female genealogy seems to be threatened by separation and the loss of contact and communication or by the danger of interdiction inscribed into the difficulty of finding a common language. This threat is evoked in the visual modulation of the artwork: the three generations of women never appear all together in one vision but are always separated in three different visual spaces. The contact between them is limited to an encounter between two in a cyclical way or in alternating phases corresponding to the linguistic displacement between them. The paradoxical risk of a communicative aphasia inscribed in this multilingual dialogue is overcome by the inter-mediate(ing) presence of the artist, as she knows both English and Arabic, the language of the others, and weaves a dialogue *entre-trois*, and by the silent yet eloquent language of love gestures. Moreover, Sedira affirms that even lack of communication brings a meaning with it: her mother's refusal to speak French is an act of rebellion and resistance against the language of the colonisers:

Lack of communication is also a way of conveying meaning. My mother never learned French properly because she wanted to show

her rejection of French language and behaviour after the war of
independence, even though she and my father lived in France for
economic reasons – North African immigrants were used as cheap
labour. They experienced a lot of racism, and my parents felt a
sense of failure that they had to bring up their children in that
culture.

(Sedira n.d.)

The rebellious silence of Sedira's mother can be considered a break
of the force field of colonialism and racism which gives voice to resistance and survival. *Mother Tongue* evokes the language of exile and
at same time the exile of language, this is a resistance to or an impossibility of total comprehension and communicative transparency that
is inscribed in the language itself. This recalls what Jacques Derrida
has described (1998) as the strangeness or inhospitality of the mother
tongue, in reference to a colonial essence of all languages, corresponding to the process of both cultural codification and linguistic colonisation. Yet, the artist seems to invite viewers to consider the possibility
of overcoming the separation from the mother tongue through love
gestures that can restore contact, communication and sense.

In a more recent series of works, Sedira turned from the expression
of the self and its border-crossing identity to the external world, the
Mediterranean landscape with its past and present passages and transits. In her photographic series *Haunted House* (2006; see Fig. 2.3),
the reference to the past that haunts the present is quite immediate.
Sedira presents a ruined house recalling a typical figure of the common
childhood imagination, usually associated with spectrality: the ruined
house is the home of the spectres, as the title itself indicates. The edifice, situated on the coast of Algeria, overlooking the sea, is part of the
decadent beauty of the city and the place where the French soldiers,
during the Algerian war of independence (1954–62), tortured Algeri-
ans suspected of being supporters of the National Liberation Front,
then threw their corpses into the sea. The innocent childhood evoca-
tions are therefore brutally displaced by the violence of the historical
facts and their material remains in the ruined archive of the present.
The image recalls a disquieting proximity between the spectres of the
past haunting the colonial house and those of today migrants crossing
the Mediterranean, many of whom are now invisible and forgotten in
the abyss of the sea, where they lie with the ruins and human debris
of the past.

Sedira's disturbing visions of the historical and geographic reality
break every neat, homogeneous and linear representation of past and

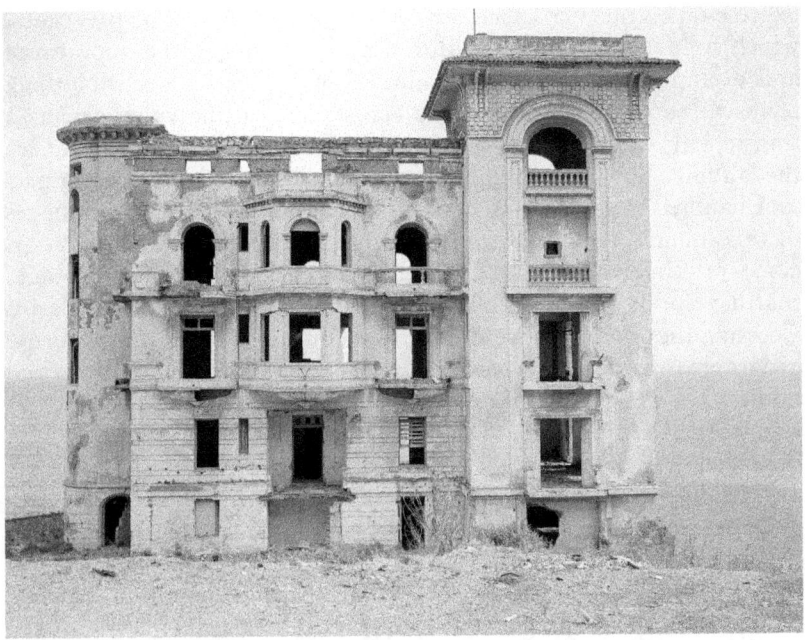

Figure 2.3 Zineb Sedira, *Haunted House III*. Colour photograph, 80×100cm, 2006.

© Zineb Sedira. Courtesy of the artist and kamel mennour, Paris

present and connect to the ambiguous, hybrid and migrant vision of the artist's transcultural self in her *Self-Portrait or The Virgin Mary*. The artist's ghostly self-portrait is connected to the cultural and historical "spectrality"' of the Mediterranean, but, while the latter can be referred to as the invisible presences concealed and silenced by the violence of colonialism and nationalism, the former provocatively recalls a different presence, destabilising, disturbing and witnessing a "past that does not pass" (Chambers, Grechi and Nash 2014).

Among Sedira's "ghostly" works centred on the Mediterranean, there is *MiddleSea* (2008). This is a single video installation, showing the journey of a man on a boat crossing the Mediterranean from Marseille to Algiers. He wanders in solitude on an almost empty boat, and his Mediterranean transit resembles a hallucination, an oneiric, dark voyage, suspended in time and space. A variety of aesthetic and expressive elements contribute to create an atmosphere of suspension, immobility and waiting: nocturnal, dark colours, a fixed apathetic expression on the man's face, strident music accompanying the scenes, which follow one another with a shading montage, the appearance and disappearance of the man himself on the boat's deck. Nothing seems to happen but the journey across the sea: the video depicts a transit without an arrival, a constant crossing of which we never see the landing. Thus what can be seen in this disturbed, disquieting passage haunted by the possibility of disappearance? Where do the images of this immobile passage transpose us? The route toward Algiers is constantly interrupted and crossed by other, invisible, past, passages that deviate its direction, provoking a space-time dilation and drift. Crossing the Mediterranean becomes a journey toward other stories, geographies, cultures, memories, a meeting with other migrations and bodies. The poetical insight of Sedira's *MiddleSea* evokes the observation by the Caribbean poet Derek Walcott (1990, bk 6, ch. XLIV, l. 7), according to which the sea is not simply a landscape but is history: the sea is an archive of fragmented histories coming from different shores and ages, which are separated and yet connected by its waters.

The visionary journey in *MiddleSea* recalls, then, other stories of sea-crossing. The histories of the Mediterranean migration between Africa and Europe remind the viewer of the Atlantic history of the African diaspora to the Americas, a constant flux of forced migration produced by the British Empire that needed a workforce in its Caribbean colonies, a process of transnational construction based on territorial looting in South America and slave trade from Africa, which Paul Gilroy has defined as the "black Atlantic" (1993). In both these histories the boat assumes a particular material and symbolic meaning and is crucial for understanding the interlacing of stories apparently distant in space and time and the link between colonialism, modernisation, globalisation and different postcolonial geographies. It is significant that Sedira's video is entirely centred on a boat, and the gloomy atmosphere, the sense of peril, tension or even loss, recall the numerous drownings that in the last decades have contributed, as Iain Chambers suggests, to a "solidification" of the sea (2008). The contemporary boats overcrowded by poor people crossing the Mediterranean recall the nineteenth-century boats crossing the Atlantic with men bought in Africa on board, sailing to British overseas plantations to become slaves. Those boats were the principal instruments by which the European colonial powers expanded their commercial traffic, starting up the process of industrialisation and modernisation. The African diaspora is an integral part of our modernity, and the boat loaded with migrants approaching the Occidental coasts becomes, as Gilroy suggests, the geographical and historical signifier through which we can reconsider the relationship between the postcolonial modernity and the colonial past. "Getting on board promises a means to reconceptualise the orthodox relationship between modernity and what passes for its prehistory. It provides a different sense of where western modernity might itself be thought to begin in the constitutive relationships with outsiders that both found and temper a self-conscious sense of Western civilization" (Chambers 2008, 17).

A deep sense of displacement also emerges from the piece *Floating Coffins* (2009; Fig. 2.4). It is a video-installation composed of fourteen screens and eight speakers and cables, through which the artist shows the images she has taken during her research on the coast of Mauritania – once a crucial place of maritime global trade, today one of the main points of departure for those seeking better opportunities. The name of the place analysed by the artist is Nouadhibou, an old fishing port and an exit point for iron ore en route to Europe and the United States, which is now the route for people migrating illegally from Africa to Europe. This is a dangerous route, preceded by a journey through the desert, then a sea crossing in unsafe boats. Evoking the desperate clandestine migrations and the overbearing arbitrariness

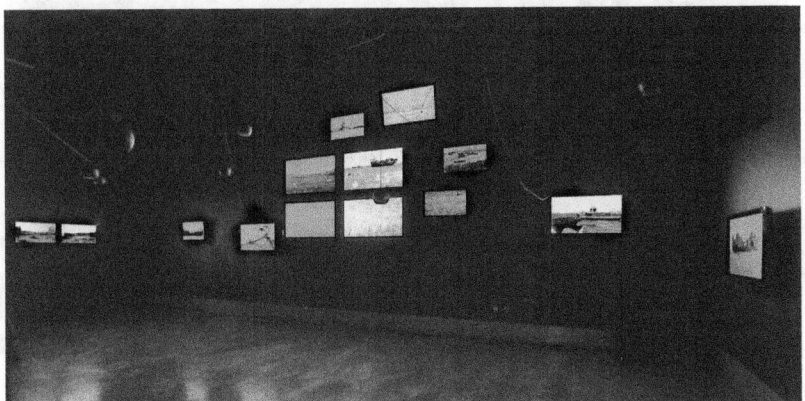

Figure 2.4 Zineb Sedira, *Floating Coffins*. Installation, 14 screens of various sizes and 8 loudspeakers, overall size dependent on space, 9 min 43 sec; soundtrack by Mikhail Karikis: view of exhibition at New Art Exchange, Nottingham, 2009. Commissioned by New Art Exchange, Nottingham.

of the global capital to which they are directly connected, Sedira draws a cemetery of boats lying on Nouadhibou's shore, now useless and excluded from international traffic. The Mauritanian seascape, similar to that of Sicily, is spread with boats whose lost functionality has transformed them into old rusty carcasses, abandoned on the waves, as floating coffins. These boats show contrasting images of mobility and immobility, through which the memory of past movements is enabled by rests and arrests, by what remains of them in the present, forever immobile. However, what emerges powerfully through each screen of the piece is a profound sense of relationality. Images of very specific places on the Mauritanian coast are gathered in a set of fragmented views, thus inscribing a sense of motion and constant reconfiguration, evoking other places, times, and histories of migration.

Sedira's maritime poetics and their insistence on the multiple connections between the Atlantic and the Mediterranean – clearly evoked also in her most recent work, *Sugar Routes* (2013; Fig. 2.5), based on

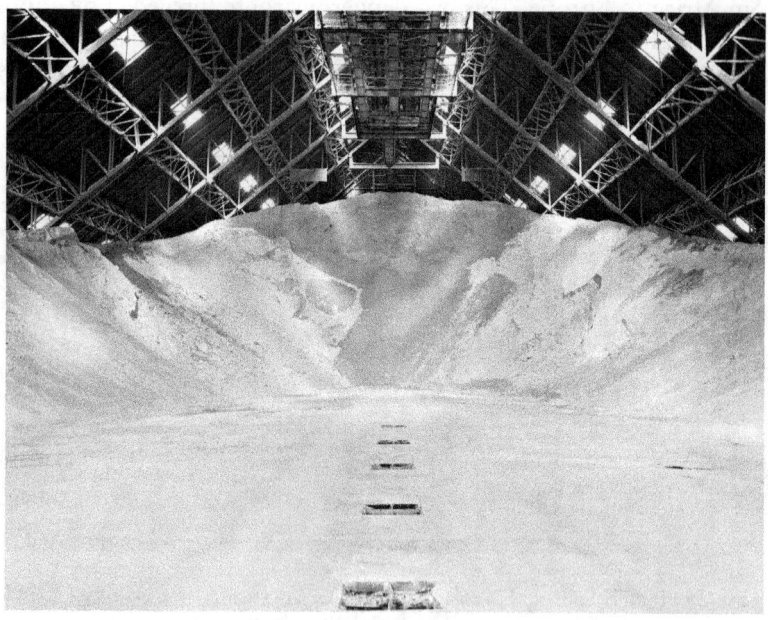

Figure 2.5 Zineb Sedira, *Sugar Routes I*. Digital C-type, 144×180 cm, 2013. Commissioned by Marseille-Provence 2013, European Capital of Culture and the Port of Marseille.

© Zineb Sedira / DACS, London. Courtesy of the artist, The Third Line, Dubai, and Plutschow Gallery, Zurich

sugar and its colonial global routes – acquire a subversive value: the artist proposes another narration of the Mediterranean and Occidental modernity, based on interlaced histories that are often submerged and silenced by the homogenising attempts of Western historiography and politics. As Lidia Curti suggests (2010), the Mediterranean region, as a place in the modern world, can be best understood as part of a mobile landscape interlaced with other places and regions in the South of the world, in new political and epistemological terms. In fact, through her exiling and estranging visions the artist invites us to consider the Mediterranean as a complex, inappropriable and interrogative space.

In the face of these unsettling visions, the colonialist will to frame and rule the cultures, identities and movements of history is destined to be frustrated. If the nation-state, as Judith Butler maintains in *Precarious Life* (2004), seeks desperately to recompose its declining sovereignty through the exaltation of strength, solidity and integrity – materially translated into the erection of walls and barriers – Sedira's "uncanny" aesthetics, undermining the idea of sovereignty itself, grant value and recognition to precariousness, to the limits of translatability and appropriation, to the right to opacity, to the self as an impure, vulnerable, excessive, disturbing presence. Here aesthetics offers an answer to the awareness of vulnerability that is diametrically opposed to the one produced by the nationalist (and masculinist) rhetoric of Western sovereignty. Rebelling against every totalitarian pretension, this aesthetic answer recognises in the partiality of the personal stories the possibility of narration itself: "without mystery, curiosity, and the form imposed by a partial answer, there cannot be stories. Just confessions, announcements, fragments of autobiographical fantasy" (Berger 1991, 71).

On the contrary, the obsession for borders, long afflicting the declining Western sovereignty, causes the people living beyond the national borders to be denied any possibility of narration. As a result they become confined to their corporeality. Here the migrant body coincides with the national border. As Federica Sossi observes, "biography is at the border, it is the residue of the person, a remnant of no interest" (2006, 133).

This denial of narration is a strategy, an obsession of power, which stems from a necessity of self-preservation and above all from a precise archival system, in conjunction with its role in the identification and arrest of unauthorized migrations. It brings people back to the traces of their passages in order to direct and block them. In this history, any space of individuality for the "borderless" is silent, "unarchived".

The archive, as the space of archivability and enunciation, the space resistant to history where narration is made possible from that which remains, is distorted by a power unable to recognise in the trace of individual life, in fragility and precariousness, any sign of positivity. As Sossi notes, erasing or letting the traces of one's self be erased, telling or letting one's self be referred to with a different name, abandoning or letting one's own past be abandoned, are the current strategies of resistance or existence against a power that no longer archives the traces of the self, but just seeks to trace them (2006, 137).

Opposed to a power that refuses to give an account of the non-archivable histories within its linear narration, Sedira's "deviant" poetics propel us toward alternative answers. Elaborating versions of the community and the self that resist the biographical capture of power, she evokes a narrative of interlaced histories, a dense plot, where an instance of change and the possibility of a historical, cultural and social reconfiguration can be recognised. A passage opens up from a sense of the world declined in the masculinist language of sovereignty, domination and imperialist power, which validates a closed ethic of bullying, to a different landscape, one based on an evocating and anti-authoritarian language and an open ethic of relationality and sustainability.

Sedira's poetics, like an enveloping veil woven with intercultural threads, unfolds strangeness and otherness. Like a story coming from afar, it narrates unexpected and unauthorized arrivals. This is a poetics that overlaps with the experience of migration itself. The artworks that the artists produce, in fact, are not simply a reproduction of reality. They are not representative but rather productive of new realities. They speak about us or with us; they touch us, they touch our senses and affect us, and thereby generate a new sensibility: a movement of feelings, images and thoughts. These pieces make us migrate and transpose us to a reality where we can recognize ourselves as "strangers to ourselves", in Julia Kristeva's words ([1988]), a condition that is now typical of the contemporary world. Through visions constantly recalling an elsewhere, we are transposed far from any sense of property, adrift, along with and beyond the artistic fruition.

Ursula Biemann's Videocartography and the Ecology of Art

The idea of a fluid, layered, contaminated and migrant geography can be reconnected to the post-humanist concept of counter-geography, elaborated by the Swiss scholar and artist Ursula Biemann in her video-essays, which she defines as "videocartographies". In the last part of this chapter, attention is focused on the political value of the relationship between art and nature. In particular, I analyse the relation between what can be considered as a border-crossing art (emerging from experiences of migration and border-crossing, displacement and the production of repositionings) and nature in the sense of a material archive of mobility. I therefore pay attention to the ways art and aesthetics articulate the relationships between matter, nature, territory and memory through a theoretical approach based on the combination of two perspectives, the postcolonial (which, as explained before, uses border-crossing thinking as a critical method) and a Deleuzian feminist materialist philosophy, with particular reference to the theoretical elaborations about nature, art, territory and movement by Elizabeth Grosz (2008). Engaging with the philosophical tradition of becoming (from the Presocratics to Spinoza and Deleuze) and with evolutionary Darwinian theory, Grosz's feminist perspective unhinges the classic opposition between nature and culture and tries to deconstruct the presumed primacy of the human over nature, established by the humanist culture:

> Nature or materiality have no identity in the sense that they are continually changing, continually emerging as new. Once we have a dynamic notion of nature, then culture cannot be seen as that which animates nature. Nature is already animated, and culture borrows its energy from nature. So it is not as if culture is the transformation of nature: culture is the fruition, the culmination of nature. Culture is no longer understood as uniquely human or as a thoroughly linguistic creation. Culture borrows from the animal. There could be no culture without an open-ended nature. An arena as culturally specific as art history or art theory owes an immense debt to the natural world.
>
> (Grosz 2005, 44)

Here nature itself is the condition of possibility for culture, it is viewed as a force that expands in matter and thought, in mind, senses and imagination, in the individual and the community, through the encounter of bodies triggering new encounters, movements, relations, transformations. "No one knows what a body can do" (Spinoza [1677]). It is notable that Spinoza here used the indefinite article, indicating that bodies are not to be restricted to human or living bodies, but to all bodies. If, then, no one knows what a body can do, this is because the assemblages into which bodies can enter are limitless.

And in entering into an assemblage or a network, the body's amount of acting is increased or diminished, assisted or checked. We can thus think of a body as being akin to a field of potentials, such that in entering into an assemblage with another body, potentials of the body are drawn or pulled forth from the body, manifesting themselves for the very first time.

Grosz underlines how the creative process (both in nature and art) is independent from any purpose or intentionality and explains how, for example, animal courtship has something intrinsically excessive and artistic, something gratuitous with respect to the mere function of survival. Similarly, art is not functional, it has nothing to do with any representative function. It does not represent that which is already given, rather it produces newness in the form of sensations and vibrations. Art and nature are transformative forces and as such they are political. They are political in themselves because they are based on differentiation, mobility, profusion and intensification of life. In this sense, Grosz refers to an "unlivable power" that passes through the body and connects human and non-human, organic and inorganic.

> Art is the most vital and direct form of impact on and through the body, the generation of vibratory waves, rhythms, that traverse the body and make the body a link with forces it cannot otherwise perceive and act upon. . . . Art is the most direct intensification of the resonance, and dissonance, between bodies and the cosmos, between one milieu or rhythm and another . . . art is the way that universe most directly intensifies life, enervates organs, mobilizes forces.
>
> (Grosz 2008, 23–4)

This is the transforming power of art, an immanent power that nonetheless goes beyond the phenomenological, beyond representation. It is possible to retrace this discourse about art and nature as processes of othering in some contemporary artworks and art experiences. This is the case of the famous silhouettes by Ana Mendieta, who used to define herself as an "earth-body" artist. Her corporeal art, a material and simultaneously spiritual practice, could be defined as a "becoming-landscape". Mendieta's body mingles with the natural elements, the land, the flowers, the trees, the fire, the water; it is there in her flesh and bones or it is evoked through its traces in the ground. The relationship between body and landscape emerges also from the photographic project by Jean Paul Bourdier and Trinh Minh-ha entitled *Bodyscapes* (2007). Both works refer to a combination and reciprocal determination of body and milieu and hence also of architecture and nature, reality and imagination. This recalls the intimate connection between nature and artifice, as for example evoked by the photographic series *Bird* (2008) by Roni Horn, where the artist plays on the perceptive and material ambiguity between human and animal.

Some examples of bio-aesthetics presented at dOCUMENTA (13) are worth citing here, such as the installation *Doing Nothing Garden* (2012) by the Chinese artist Song Dong, consisting of a grassy hill in front of the Fredericianum Museum, where seemingly nothing happens, as the artwork's title suggests, but actually a life in ferment is hidden beneath the surface, inside, out of sight, activated by the composting material which constitutes the living core of that hill. A field of action and revolution, a territory of living movement, almost invisible, as is the case in another installation, *The Lover* (2012) by the German artist–biologist Kristina Buch, consisting of a garden that, through the daily care of the artist herself, favours the creative process between the flowers and the butterflies hosted there. The fence of nettles and thistles delimiting the garden suggests that the artistic experience of nature implies a desire of border-crossing that concerns not only the physical space but also visual and perceptual limits. Besides evoking an interlacing between visible and invisible, action and inertia, art and artifice, these artworks, in their transitory and impermanent nature, recall the fact that nature can be understood as a living archive of bodies in transit and migrant matter, as an uncontrollable space of border-crossings and hybridisations, which produce life and death. The human is only one of the different bodies that participate in the material plane of composition, in a web of relations and assemblages that cannot be reduced to dynamics of inferiority and superiority, even when the creative process concerns knowledge.

As Ursula Biemann observes, human beings are not the only privileged subjects of knowledge because what they know and practise is part of a "hybrid ecology" (Biemann 2014). This is what Biemann articulates in her work *Egyptian Chemistry* (2011), which consists of a collection of videos where she explores the hybrid ecology of the Nile, that is, the coalescence of water and other organic, natural elements with human, social and technological components. The project is based on fieldwork where water samples were taken in sixteen locations along the Nile and around the delta wetlands. Their chemistry was analysed and the locations documented in their socio-ecological configuration.

The focus is understandably on human achievement. But if we see past such anthropocentric visions, we have to admit that indeed, humans have used the force of the Nile, but so have lazy fish, suspended pollutants, ammonium nitrate, cement factories, and wheat crops, all of which have their say in the video. The river has to be thought of as a hybrid interactive system that has always been organic, technological and social all at once. The Nile is like a machine with enormous potential natural agency – electric, genetic, chemical, thermal; a comprehensive expression of nature's capacity to produce energy.

(Biemann 2014, 211)

In a series of short videos, *Egyptian Chemistry* brings knowledge from multiple sources – from atmospheric physics to hydraulic modelling, peasant activism, agro-science, metaphysics and ecology – into a single forum, forming an epistemogram or a sort of epistemological cartography. This is the production of an ecological paradigm in stark opposition to the neo-liberal, capitalist one produced by the Egyptian government.

The core motif in *Egyptian Chemistry* is the collection of water samples taken by a young Egyptian at specific sites along the Nile, some of them rural, some industrial, others urban. Another video, directly related to the first one, documents the same young Egyptian, this time in a white coat, as he brings the Nile water samples into the installation of *Egyptian Chemistry* at the Contemporary Art Forum in Alexandria where he rebottles them in chemistry-laboratory glasses. Each sample represents an archive of multiple histories where human and non-human realities emerge in a variety of formations. Biemann underlines the extraordinary but often neglected proximity between scientific naturalism and social sciences, but also between nature, chemistry and poetry, aesthetics and the mythic imagination. It is not by chance that she uses the word *al khemia* to describe her aesthetic and epistemological approach:

This more wholesome approach goes back to an ensemble of practices encompassing chemical, biological, metallurgical and philosophical dimensions, represented by the original name of "Al Khemia", long before the epistemological division into disciplines and subdisciplines set in. Al Khemia happened to be the ancient word for Egypt, meaning the Black Land, possibly due to the muddy Nile floods periodically fertilising the land. The term alludes to the vision that, before anything else, the earth is a mighty chemical body where the crackling noise of the forming and breaking of molecular bonds can be heard at all times.

(Biemann 2014, 217)

Egyptian Chemistry confronts us with a living archive of hybrid matter and a hybrid consciousness of the world. It may represent an invitation to consider the possibility of an alternative cartography of reality as well as a new archive, able to account for a different humanism, a different political economy. The archives of the future should be able to register, as Biemann's video-essay suggests, the elements of an untameable and unrepresentable ecology that reconnects to life as difference, unfolding from the encounter between nature and culture, *bios* and *zoe*, matter and technology, chemistry and magic.

The hybrid ecology of reality suggests epistemologic and economic paradigms which are often in radical conflict with the current ones. By contrast, the ecofuturist video *The Radiant* presented at dOCUMENTA (13) by the Otolith Group explores the dystopian landscape of Fukushima after the nuclear disaster. What is most striking here is the almost total absence of bodies, of living beings, both human and animal, an absence evoking the danger of extinction produced by nuclear energy. What is important here is not a *memento mori* effect nor a moralistic recall of our finitude or death, as it is after all part of the vital cycle and process of "becoming other", or, as Rosi Braidotti puts it, of a "becoming imperceptible" (2006). The critical point pertains instead to what can be defined as a politics of death, characteristic of both our past and present political economy. This can be referred to as a "necropolitics", the term used by Achille Mbembe to describe the racist colonial power as a force that exchanges life for death and death for life, and which is responsible for the violence, abuses, silences, absences and gaps on which modernity has been constructed, and which still largely remain buried in institutional archives (Mbembe 2008).

The encounter with art and the natural and historical archives brings us into another encounter with a certain impact: for, more than an encounter, it is actually a challenge. This is represented by post-humanism as a cultural and political project that brings directly into focus our colonial past and its role in the construction of the asymmetrical and oppositional relationships between human and animal, history and nature and our postcolonial present, in its various forms (migratory processes, critique, theory, aesthetics, ethics), positing the possibility of a reparation and reconfiguration of those ruined relations.

The Matri-Archive of the Mediterranean

Inspired by a multiple, complex and plural vision of the Mediterranean and by the archive understood as a space of dwelling, wandering and narration and simultaneously the space of creative and political intervention is the project, *Matri-Archive of the Mediterranean: Graphics and Matters* (*MAM*), carried out by a group of researchers, including me, from the University of Naples "L'Orientale".[3] The project consists of a web platform dedicated to the archiving and dissemination of the contemporary aesthetics and languages, or according to our definition, "graphics and matters", the signs and traces of expression – visual arts, plastic arts, photography, dance, music, land-art, bio-art – produced by female artists of the Mediterranean area. This digital archive is the technical and operational result of an investigation of the archive from a culturalist and postcolonial perspective, recalling Stuart Hall's definition of "post-museum" (2001) and Jacques Derrida's concept of a new technologic *chora* inscribed in the archiving practice (1995), a virtual meeting space of multiple stories, memories, places, subjectivities, often repressed and silenced by the official archives. The archive here has been articulated and developed according to a gender connotation (*matri*) and a geographical specification (the Mediterranean).

The interpretative assumption of the project is that, in contemporary times, the archival vocation is essential: a *mal d'Afrique*, a *mal d'archive*. We all love archiving – in order to remember or to forget – and the archive, its desire or its compulsion, is always linked to the *arké* (Carotenuto 2012) to the archons, to the architecture of a place destined to the consignment, in patriarchal lineage, of a selectivity of texts, signs, memories, documents and materials operated by – male – guardians working for the interests of the – male – institutions which are meant to safeguard memory / from memory. The existing form of the archive is male, patriarchal and patrilineal: the hereditary of what repeats, safeguards and archives order, power and tradition.

The question that gave birth to the matri-archive resounds for difference. What happens if, instead, differently from the patri-archive, an archive is instituted and devoted to women, to the ones who have been – and still are – excluded by the selectivity of the male archive? What changes if, and when, the archive practices a transmission of knowledge in feminine lineage? If the archons becomes "woman", "matriarch", offering the accumulation and dissemination of a female knowledge? *MAM* – a new, potential, virtual archive of a maternal, liquid, migrant, natural, technical, material memory, preserved and transmitted in contemporary times by the aesthetics and performances of Mediterranean female artists – poses these and many more questions

---

3 www.matriarchiviomediterraneo.org.

and issues, connecting them to four privileged archiving themes: the Matriarchs, *la Mer*, the Matrix, Matter.

The time and space of intervention of *MAM* are vast and immemorial – it can extend to the mythological and contemporary figurations of the Mediterranean women, the Matriarchs, which look back to the myth and forward to today's myths. They are terrifying and enchanting Medusas, young Koras and Persephones, tragic Antigones showing another sense of existence through their claims for a right to asylum and burial that, propelling us beyond the necropolitical regime of today, would change the destiny of the entire world. These feminine figurations rewrite a female genealogy and *puissance* (Cixous 1976) that emerges from the Mediterranean maternal waters (the sea is also *la Mer*, in assonance with "the mother"), tormented by hostility, wars and failures, in order to liberate their chants of life. The contemporary sea of migrations while marked by the many signs of death, shipwrecks, dispersions, missed arrivals and infinite exiles, is at the same time, touched by the many signs of life constituted by the creative passion, which affirms the movement, the freedom, the experimentation, the courage, the journey, the inventive re-elaborations of art through new rhythms, visions, dances, drawings. Here the images offered by one of the many mothers of *MAM*, the French–Algerian artist Zineb Sedira, in her works devoted to the Mediterranean Sea, are strongly evocative. Abandoned ships, rusted carcasses, harbours, marine paths, one-way signs, exiles without return and, together, the performative celebrations of the "lighthouses" which, in this liquid space that brings death and life at the same time, illuminate the necessary journey to undertake, by recording the – colonial/postcolonial – traces of memory, in order to transform them into signs of the future. Like a "lighthouse" à la Sedira, *MAM* proposes to "gather" (a word of deconstructive resonance) the feminine graphics of an archaic and ancient intelligence, which is at the same time, modern (a modernity "different" from the canonical Western male lineage), contemporary, experiential, made of infinite forms and different directions.

The artworks hosted in this alternative female archive are conceived as a "boundary event" (Minh-ha 2005), that is, a process of differentiation and a practice of memory that recalls the question of borders and belonging, the expropriation and reappropriation of space. They reflect the feminist politics of location of the self (Rich 1985), where the subjectivity is thought of as embodied, historical, immanent, yet mutable and multiform, and is evoked here through a poetics of border-crossing and translation. This political and philosophical stance invests also the idea of a Matrix, in creative and critical ways. The main connotations of the feminine have been historically identified with mother nature and the mother tongue: the natural and the original in binary opposition to the technique, the artificial, the material. Contrasting these dialectics of Occidental thought, *MAM* claims the power of a Matrix who interrogates herself about the origin and belonging of femininity to "Mother Nature" and consigns herself into the care of the natural elements as a space of creative encounters and transformation in the preservation and dissemination of the "Mother Tongue". The desired, yet never fully possessed tongue (Derrida 1998), configured in her inventive contaminations and in the encounter with *techné*, the languages and techniques of the contemporary performances where a corporeal, carnal, sensorial aesthetics is sustained and emphasised by technological experimentations. A different form of archive can be thus produced for registering and remembering the body's poetic gesture, and even a different law of gravity can be elaborated, as for example, Isabel Rocamora's videos seems to indicate. Her veiled dancers in the desert and its constant transformative movement of sand and wind escape from the weight of bodily gravity, affirming poetically a subtraction, a suspension, and a refusal of the constraints that patriarchal society has imposed on the female body.

The encounter between *techné* and the body marks the female active deconstruction of the fundamental oppositions of occidental thought and the archive that celebrates it: the natural against the technological, the origin opposed to the future, thus generating, as for destiny, a passion of *MAM* for Matter. This is a "platform" offered for the interaction and processual analysis of the "questions" that constellate an archive of female difference and the questions of the materials that, more than ever, require the invention of alternative and sustainable practices of conservation and recycling of the Mediterranean women's cultural and artistic heritage. This section is dedicated to the feminist theoretical debate about the relationship between culture and nature (Barad 2012; Grosz 2005; Haraway 2007; Preciado 2013), and to bio-art / land-art / eco-art where the use, reuse, recycling of the waste materials, the artistic experimentations and the border-crossings (of disciplines, geographies, materials, bodies, species) interrogate the relationship between culture and nature, humanity and animality, chemistry and artifice, technology and ecology, recognising a molecular contamination of reality and the queerness and alterity residing at the heart of m-other nature. In this sense, the project's aim is to curate the artworks of the women who contaminate the disciplines of art and humanism with those of science and technology in order to explore the possibility of a creative recycling of approaches, methodologies, ideas, matters, bodies and practices of knowledge open to alternative modes of inhabiting the contemporary and the future times and spaces.

The last case-study I will analyse here is directly connected to *MAM* and the postcolonial Mediterranean. It is *Il paese delle terre d'Oltremare* ("The Land of the Overseas Territories") (Cianelli 2014a; see Fig. 2.6), an artistic and research project elaborated by the Neapolitan artist Alessandra Cianelli, in collaboration with Beatrice Ferrara, two of the "matriarchs" that nurture *MAM*. The project, constantly in progress, opens up the (post)colonial archive of Italy through the guide of a critical wonder, like Alice in Wonderland (as evoked by the title), and a subverted exotic desire for discovery, assumed as a research methodology with a "fabulous power" that is able to "open hidden, disappeared, or never existed lands" (Cianelli 2014a, 1).

The project aims at "discovering", gathering and interlacing sounds, images, objects, words and memories linked to the stories of "the overseas", that is the Italian colonial territories beyond the Mediterranean,

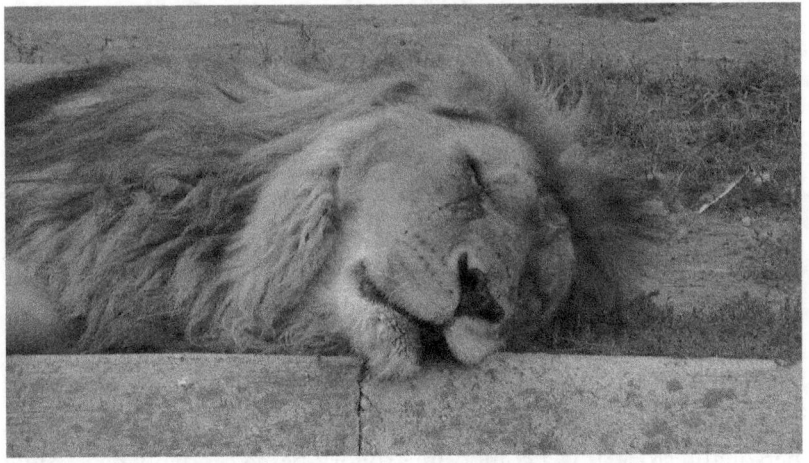

Figure 2.6 Alessandra Cianelli, *Gli sguardi amorosi riaprono gli occhi dei dormienti chiusi dal passato insolente* [Loving Glances Open the Sleepers' Eyes Shut by an Insolent Past]. Video still, 2012–15. From *Il paese delle terre d'Oltremare* [The Land of the Overseas Territories].

© Alessandra Cianelli. Courtesy of the artist

Cyrenaica (Libya, Albania), and the Horn of Africa (Ethiopia, Soma-
lia, Eritrea), known in the Fascist period as Italian Oriental Africa. In
particular, the investigation is based on research conducted in Naples
at what can be considered as its most emblematic colonial institution: the Triennial Exhibition of the Overseas Territories, the place
where the project converges and diverges. The Fascist architecture, the
"exotic" animal and botanical presences in the exhibition, as well as a
seemingly inaccessible institutional archive, are all that remains of the
colonial past of the city and the central role it played in that enterprise.
Naples, during the culminating years of the imperial period, was the
port from which the colonial ships sailed and the seat of the University
of Naples "L'Orientale" where the colonial functionaries were formed.
As the first capital of the South colonised by the northern Italian/Savoy
reign, Naples was destined to become the seat of the Ministry of the
Colonies and, in its turn, the northern capital of the southern lands
conquered in Africa, thus concluding the vicious colonialist circle of
subordination and integration. With the collapse of Fascism and the
subsequent ideological condemnation, this project has failed miser-
ably and its history has been buried deep in the collective and personal
unconscious.

It is exactly in the shadow of these colonial ruins that Cianelli moves,
recalling the "neofuturist and fantaexotic imaginary" (2014a, 2) that
had nurtured the colonial project and the Exhibition of the Overseas
Territories, along with her personal insights, memories and fantasies.
The artist's investigation touches on the relationship between her family and colonial history, starting by interrogating and questioning the
familiarity of some words whose meaning seems to be forgotten. Their
survival is left only to their sound, and their resignification is hidden
in the emotive and sensorial memory of the body that "registered"
or experienced it. The words transformed into sound suddenly reveal
their hidden and forgotten meaning. Thus, Cianelli's video, *Parole che
(si) nascondono* ("Words that Hide / are Hidden") (2012), is a "mini-
mal attempt", as the artist herself says, at giving an account of the
Italian colonial presence in Africa, its persistence in the cultural and
political unconscious of contemporary Italy and its reverberations in a
personal history. It is a composite artwork based on two videos: *Sulle
spalle* ("On my Back") (Fig. 2.7) and *Ambaradam* ("Confusion"),
both produced within the *Il paese delle terre d'Oltremare* project.
The first video, which is also hosted by *MAM*, revolves around the
repressed memory of the artist's grandfather, enrolled by the Fascist
army in the war for the defence of the colonised territories in Cyrenaica and killed in 1940 during British bombing. A story removed

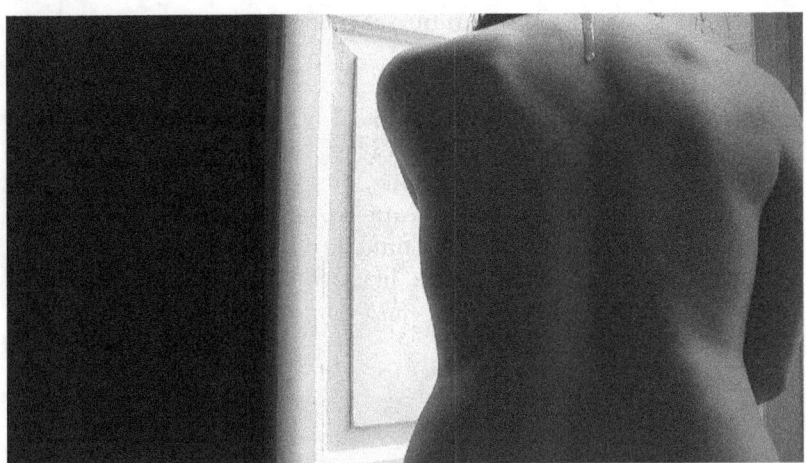

Figure 2.7 Alessandra Cianelli, *Sulle spalle* [On my Back]. Video still, 2012.
© Alessandra Cianelli. Courtesy of the artist

from the family memories, where the Fascist censorship ends by over-lapping and invading the personal narrations and existence. Beyond the violence of the silence imposed by (his)tory, the artist makes this story live again through the female voices: she consigns the narration to her mother who reads the letters written by her father, during the war. The second video, *Ambaradam*, like the first, follows the meaning of the words concealed under the sound, mixing reality and fiction, familiar and unfamiliar, innocence and guilt, play and war, joy and sorrow. In Italian, the word *ambaradan* is generally used to indicate confusion, turmoil, chaos; it can also recall a magic formula or a dog-gerel sang by children. This apparently playful word also recalls a terrible event linked to Italian incursions into the Horn of African. Amba Aradam is an Ethiopian mountain that was the bloody theatre of the Italian colonial campaign for Ethiopia, which was annexed to the Fascist empire in 1936. The African name has entered common use in Italian language to indicate chaos, but the historical meaning it unconsciously evokes has been removed and concealed. As Cianelli suggests, the word has been transformed in order to assume a more convenient meaning (2014b, 165).

The Mediterranean here appears once again to be a meeting point of the words and memories lost between its shores, a place of historical awakening and re-enactment, a space of critical cuts and desiring encounters, of past ruins and future challenges:

> This is the land where I search for an external legitimisation of my internal journey. The broken roots, my mother, a secret, a place, the abandonment, the exclusion; being out of place, on the border, being a threshold and an opening.
>
> This is the way you can learn Nostalgia and Betrayal: backwards, forwards, around the time, I, me, present and cutting, in order to catch past and future, like two birds with one stone.
>
> (Cianelli 2014b, 166)

3 Installations
Heritage, Belonging and Out-of-Place Legacies

Lara Baladi's Heterotopic Landscapes

Art, according to Grosz's theory mentioned above, is movement, crossing of spaces and territories, breaking of any system of closure and deterritorialisation. Art cuts and frames a part of chaos from chaos; it captures fragments of the living matter of the world and releases a multiplicity of new sensations and vibrations. Art connects to the body and connects the body to the world's chaos; it works like a porous frame that creates a provisional delimitation, a momentous territorialisation, "in order to retouch chaos" (Grosz 2008, 7)

This vision is what Lara Baladi's digital collages seem to recall. Baladi is a Lebanese artist and photographer, living between Cairo and the United States, educated in Paris and London, then in Beirut, where she is among the leading members of the famous photographic archive and research centre, Arab Image Foundation. Her collages seem to connect us to the chaos of the world, capturing it in little pieces of images linked to other parts of the world, each fragment recalling another one, in a constant process of correlation and layering that territorialises and at the same time deterritorialises the sense of each part. Baladi's aesthetics, as well as Grosz's theory, recall the idea of counter-space or heterotopy, elaborated by Foucault:

> There are also, and this probably in all cultures, all civilisation, real places, effective places, places that are written into the institution of society itself, and that are a sort of counter-emplacements, a sort of effectively realised utopia, in which the real emplacements, all the other emplacements that can be found within culture, are simultaneously represented, contested and inverted; a kind of place that are outside all places, even though they are actually localizable. Since these places are absolutely other than all

the emplacements that they reflect, and of which they speak, I shall call them, by way of contrast to utopias, heterotopias.

(Foucault [1967], 4)

Baladi's collages, recalling the intercultural and "nomad" biography of the artist, disturb language and bring to the surface the explosion of the sense in infinite pieces, drawing chaos from chaos, making visible the fact that the sense of the world, life and identity is not an effect of rootedness, depth and closure. Rather, as Gilles Deleuze maintains, it is a sense of eradication, what he calls "effect of surface" or the "Carroll effect". Making reference to Lewis Carroll's *Alice's Adventures in Wonderland*, Deleuze explores a different logic of common sense as being composed of direction and location ([1969], 4). Against what the classical and modern philosophical traditions affirmed, Deleuze does not seek to find sense in the secret abyss of man's soul or in the mysteries of God or in transcendental laws. The sense "stops being Principle, Reservoir, Preserve, Origin" (Deleuze [1969], 60). It stops being an absolute alterity but is rather a relative and relational one: a continuity between inside and outside, up and down, forward and backward; an Alice-like continual passage from one surface to the other, "through the looking glass" rather than remaining enchanted in its reflection. Alice's tumble, therefore, consists of an ascent to the surface, a disavowal of depth – "depth unfolds on / as width, the deep stops being a compliment" ([1969], 187) – recognising that everything happens on the border of reality and common sense. Similarly, according to Grosz's vision, art does not aim at showing, manifesting, representing anything, but rather it produces new sensations and corporeal energy, thus creating the possibility of becoming other.

An analogy is at play here between this logic of sense as becoming other and Baladi's artistic nomadic figurations and in particular her collage *Oum el Dounia* ("Mother of the Earth"), inspired by the myth of creation and Lewis Carroll's famous novel reconfigured through an Orientalist perspective. In *Oum el Dounia*, Carroll's characters overlap with Orientalist images, which now represent stereotypes of Egyptian culture. The title of the work, "Mother of the Earth", is, for instance, the name of Egypt par excellence. The wood where Alice loses her way is replaced by the desert, similarly peopled by "queer" and mutant subjects. In the middle of the desert there is the sphinx, and the Nile Delta is drawn in papyrus, as in reproductions made for tourists. Everywhere there are the same characters that Alice bumps into, but here they are "hybrid". The Queen of Hearts is a Bedouin walking with a turkey on a leash; a mermaid, her tail reminiscent of odalisque veils, is outstretched on the dunes. The Caterpillar on his mushroom is a shell-man wearing a fez and smoking *shisha*; the White Rabbit, symbolizing fertility and time, has become a plush toy, transformed into its artificial counterpart. Moreover, the majority of the characters are drawn asleep, as is the case with Alice herself, under the palms, in a general ambiguity between dream and reality, as well as between East and West.

Creation and nonsense: the ordering principle of reality, of regulation and establishment of the confines between sky and earth, between the mineral, the vegetal, the animal, the human, between dimensions of space and time, is put in relation with its opposite: the principle of indifferentiation and the intermingling of differences. Through an Orientalist dislocation of Alice's story, Baladi appropriates the destabilizing power of Carroll's paradoxes, extending their purchase beyond the geographical, cultural and historical boundaries of the original text: a literary text is turned into a visual one, a cultural product of the British colonial era becomes a transcultural, postcolonial aesthetic work.[1] The materials of collage, the artist's privileged artistic technique, is here philosophy and culture.

Significantly, Baladi's artwork itself is characterised by a series of transformations, by a perpetual becoming other, from a medium to the other, and a city to the other. In 2001 Baladi displayed her work on the streets of Cairo, in the form of big billboards of a movie, like the many in every city in the world, characterising the contemporary urban scenario. The work became the fictional propaganda of a movie that did not exist, playing on the mix between fiction and reality. Some writings say: "you, me, and everybody in *Oum el Dounia*" to suggest how people passing by are spectators and at the same time actors of that film. It is directed by Baladi, with a double reference to the artist's name and its Arabic meaning, "our land", indicating that the plot is defined by the details and events surrounding people. The displacement of the artwork in the urban space implies a displacement of perception

---

1 Written during the Victorian age, when Egypt became a British colony, Lewis Carroll's book is a brilliant satire of Victorian society, its institutions, manners, education and literature, but not its colonial enterprise. The fact that the critical instance represented by Lewis's book investigates questions concerning general morality, social hypocrisy, political corruption and abuse, without considering the violence and abuses external to the British territory but directly connected to it, shows how the idea of a British political, social, cultural and economical supremacy was naturalised, and how such illusion contributed to legitimate the colonial conquest.

and meaning concerning both the city, its inhabitants and "our land". As happens to Alice in the wood, walking in the city implies the possibility of being disoriented and transformed by the encounter with the unexpected coming from elsewhere. The work enters into what Iain Chambers defines as a "language of mobile constellations", which characterizes the postcolonial metropolis, that is into a migrant landscape that invests and re-configures the ordinary sense, "thus opening a breach into the familiar" (Chambers 1997, 92).

In 2006, Baladi conceived and organized an unusual excursion in the Egyptian desert. A group of thirty people, among them artists, journalists, writers, various activists, all coming from different parts of the world, spent seven days in the desert. Every two days they moved from one spot to another. The people involved in this project, called *Fenenim el-Rahhal*, which means "Nomadic Artists", were invited to experience the crossing of the desert as creative nomadism. According to the curator Simon N'jami, they participated in an experience more focused on process than accomplishment, which aimed at rebuilding what binds human beings alike, all the while facing, without qualm or fear, what makes human beings unalike. During the rests in the tent, equipped with all the necessary supplies, the participants visualized the attendant artist's artworks, and discussed some themes inspired by nomadism, art making and the eastern desert. The desert was considered not as a sort of void land, or *terra nullius*; rather, in the light of its historical meaning, as the crucial space of border-crossing, cultural intersection, commercial exchange and the point where Northern Africa and Sub-Saharan Africa, as well as Africa and Europe, meet. The desert becomes the clue, which leads to rethinking such notions as "identity" and "territoriality", underlining the importance that art may have in this relation. In fact, the contemporary artist embodies the nomadic spirit of the Bedouins: in perpetual movement around the world to make and exhibit her/his creations, aware of the fact that there is no place removed from the chaos of the world. Finally, in 2007 Baladi presented her work as a big tapestry exhibited at Brancolini-Grimaldi Gallery in Rome, concretising in the many knots of the new work the multiple frames and passages of her experiences. In Baladi's aesthetics the creative activity becomes one with this chaotic context, and such becoming is an event taking place in the re-elaboration of memory.

The theory of relations elaborated by Édouard Glissant acquires here particular relevance, underlining the productive and creative sense of mixture, errancy and memory. In *Poetics of Relations* ([1990]), Glissant starts from the example of the geographical and historical experience of the Africans and West Indians caught up in the trans-atlantic web of the slave trade and maintains that even such a terrible experience as slavery can produce specific forms of knowledge and agency able to cut across the dark shadow of that experience. In other words, Glissant recognizes relations as fundamentally important, even when they come out of traumatic circumstances, underlining also the importance of the centre or of being located in the middle, that is, being culturally and ethnically hybrid. According to Glissant the deadly potential of historical violence and abuse can be reduced or even transformed positively. The memory of a painful experience like that of slavery and forced integration into the coloniser's culture, as it happened to the Caribbean people, can acquire a subversive dimension through a valorisation of the minoritarian and rhizomatic becoming of blacks, Creoles, and the descendants of slaves and the colonised. Unlike the European colonisers, attached to a unitary and universal vision of identity which even legitimates as "civilising" the enterprises of colonial conquest, the people, languages and cultures that grow in the middle, like the rhizome, generate a multiplicity of belonging, a proliferation of differences and minorities, where the vitality of human (and non human) biodiversity or the "echoes of the world" reverberate. The poetics of relation is a form of philosophic nomadism that underlines the importance of being in-between as an ontology of non-unity, non-pureness, non-origin. It reconnects to the living chaos of the world and the possibilities of transformation that are inscribed in it.

In this sense, Baladi's art and its accent on chaos and connectivity allows the possibility of inhabiting a space of intermittences and movements between different cultures, a hybrid space of living and relating to the world alternatively. The process of composition inherent in the works Baladi produces, the cut and paste of images, the solicitations coming from their rich visual grammar, elude the risk of closure and reduction to the same, unfolding an aesthetics of critical nomadism and relationality that is directly immersed into the events of the world.[2]

---

2 In this sense, Lara Baladi's recent artistic projects are particularly significant for their political engagement. For example, Tahrir Radio and Tahrir Cinema, founded during the 2011 Egyptian popular revolutions, were conceived as archival and narrative support for that political and social experience. Baladi used the collected material in the development of another research project, *Vox Populi: Archiving a Revolution in the Digital Age*, funded by MIT, dedicated to the digital archives and their ephemeral nature, and aimed at the creation of a multimedia document. See opendoclab.mit.edu/lara-baladi.

Mona Hatoum's Displacing Maps

In the aesthetics of the Beirut-born, London-based, Palestinian artist Mona Hatoum, the exploration of the relation between place, space, identity and memory is profoundly informed by the experiences of exile, displacement and the multiple languages and cultures to which the artist is differently related. Far from promoting itself as representative of a people, a land or a history, Hatoum's art evokes the heterogeneous, differential, vertiginously ambiguous nature of an identitarian in-betweenness, that can clearly be referred to the artist's lived experiences but also concerns life experience as such. Hence, Hatoum's art simultaneously evokes the risk of being too strongly rooted in our "home", recalling Edward Said's observation that "borders and barriers, which enclose us within the safety of our familiar territory, can also become prisons" (2000b, 185).

The child of Palestinian exiles in Lebanon during the Deir Yassin carnage in 1948, Mona Hatoum was in London when the Israeli army occupied Lebanon and civil war broke out in 1982. Like her parents, she is now exile in a foreign land, uprooted from her home. In one of her first works, the video-installation *Corps étranger* (1994), she explores herself as a foreign body, constantly and multiply displaced. It is in the "geography closest-in" (Rich 1985, 9) of her body that the artist finds the signs of the inseparable bond between the familiar and the foreign that characterises both her biography and her aesthetics. The work involves the spectator in a sort of voyage exploring the artist's interior body, through images obtained by endoscopic techniques. The work plays with ideas and sensations of being a foreign body and its multiple identification with both the artist's disquieting intimacy, the camera introduced into her body and the spectator's voyeuristic look. Enlarged images of the artist's body are projected onto the floor of a womb-like cylindrical structure which hosts the spectator. The latter, in turn, finds him- or herself projected into a visual map of the human form, surfing from the surface of the eyes, hair and skin to its internal cavities and their wet and palpitant walls, bloody membranes and mucosa, with the amplified rhythm of the heart and breath as a soundtrack.

Hatoum invites the spectator to look at the body from an unusual perspective, highlighting how the most intimate site, once made public and amplified, can even acquire a disrupting power. In fact, while the observer's position seems to dominate vision, it is actually dominated by a condition of reclusion since vision is permitted uniquely by entering the cylindrical space, which contains and simultaneously engulfs the spectator. Desa Philippi observes how this work triggers ambiguous analogies with some contrasting stereotypes about femininity – on the one hand woman as passive object of the male gaze, on the other she is also seen as a devouring monster, *vagina dentata*, sphinx (Philippi 1999, 367). *Corps étranger* involves and encloses the viewer on multiple levels: personal, physical and geographical. The voyage into the entrails has also a particular significant historical connotation if we consider the artist memories of her mother's accounts about the Deir Yassin massacre, during which pregnant women were dismembered.

Hatoum's body images recall both the multiple geography of her biography and the fragmented lives evoked by her mother. Some powerful and critical relations with the world unfold here. As Volker Adolphs observes, in Hatoum's art the body appears as vulnerable, fragmented, violated and at the same time whole, strong, menacing, like an interface between the internal and external reality, the personal and collective experience, the intimate and alien dimension: "the body is no less alien, unstable, and insecure than the world itself; an unexplorable landscape, a bounded space that is both protective shell and inescapable prison, a boundless expanse that is both liberating and frightening" (Adolphs 2004, 59).

The culture and geopolitics of closure, confinement and the building of walls is impiously questioned by Hatoum's aesthetics of border-crossing. This is particularly evident in the different maps the artist has produced, of both Palestine and the world, blurring any distinction between closeness and distance, familiarity and strangeness. The memory of a "double vision", of simultaneous dimensions and overlapping territories, is impressed in Hatoum's cartography. In an interview with artist Janine Antoni, Hatoum declared her difficulty in establishing neat borders of her cultural belonging: "I'm often asked the same question, 'what in your works come from your culture?' As if I have a recipe and I can actually isolate the Arab ingredient, the woman ingredient, the Palestinian ingredient. People often expect tidy definitions of otherness, as if identity is something fixed and easily definable" (Antoni 1998, 57).

Time and space are inseparable, as in *Present Tense* (1996), which reproduces a map of the occupied territories to be returned to the Palestinians drawn up at the Oslo Peace Agreement of 1993. Exhibited at the Anadiel Gallery, East Jerusalem, it consists of a grid of soap blocks, placed on the floor, like a carpet, on whose surface small red glass beads are impressed, like blood drops, to delineate the land borders. The process of restitution has never taken place, Yasser Arafat having refused to sign an agreement involving a map he was not allowed to see. In the secret, unilateral maps and projects of Israel and the United States is inscribed an imperialist desire of exclusive decision and possession, and a nexus between cartography, the constitution of property and colonial power, as Irit Rogoff underlines:

> Maps make property – they do so through . . . laws, contracts, treaties, indices, covenants as well as plain old deals. Following on this same logic maps produce the "Law" . . . through the establishment of such parameters as "the border" which sustains division between those privileged with rights and those outside of them.
>
> (Rogoff 2000, 75)

Hatoum draws maps too, but nothing in them corresponds to the colonial logic of division and control; rather, they recall the dangerous desire of free movement. Significantly, the soap functioning as a map in *Present Tense* is a traditional artisanal product of Nablus, whose fabrication has never stopped, even in wartime. For this, and also for its provisional materiality, it functions as a symbol of resistance against the barriers of power: the soap is destined to melt, washing away those bloody borderlines encapsulated in an eternal present.

Hatoum's predilection for evanescent and slipping materials to make maps with is emblematic. Her *Map* (1998) consists of a big glass carpet, made of small clear marbles delineating the world map. But the high fidelity of the reproduction is under constant threat. A false step, a light touch, even the most imperceptible vibration of the floor is sufficient to decompose the territorial coordinates. This is a map with unstable borders, yet insidious, as the possibility of losing balance and falling down can hardly be avoided. The idea of decomposition of borders as an effect of movement is also what seems to emerge from the installation *Continental Drift* (2000). Here the fragile stability of the terrestrial surface, once again made of glass, is constantly menaced by the sea, consisting of thin layer of iron filings, ruffled by a rotating magnetic arm placed below the work's circular structure. The viewer has the sense that the iron wave could shatter the continental borders, thus irremediably altering the world's physiognomy. Hatoum's land is constantly adrift under the inevitable erosive action of fluxes and movements, and their unpredictable effects. This artwork, like the more recent *Shift* (2012), evokes Jean Baudrillard's observation that "there is no more system of reference to tell us what happened to *the geography of things.* We can only take a geoseismic view" (1987, 127). Hatoum inaugurates a new system of reference that questions the solidity of the land beneath our feet, where it seems impossible to plant and cultivate the roots of belonging. This "new geography of things" is rather rhizomatic, to use a metaphor dear to Deleuze and Guattari ([1980]): it crosses borders, tears off the roots, stirs the codes, composed, as it is, of spaces of both dispersion and convergence, deterritorialisation and territorialisation, of folds, fluxes, currents, vapours. Rather than relying on fixed points, beyond any logic of precision and "establishment", Hatoum's maps display what is rendered invisible by official cartography: the experience of geography, the personal geography of a life-path showing the precariousness of borders and the decomposition of spaces, a "subversive" route that leads to the threshold between the known and the unknown, the familiar and the untimely, the proper and the improper, exceeding any clear correspondence between territorial delimitation and identitarian identification. This relation between geography and biography is often, emblematically, recurrent in Hatoum's art.

The map *Projection* (2006) reproduces in two different kinds of paper-pulp the perimeters of the continents according to the cartographic projections elaborated by the historian Arno Peters in 1973, reconfiguring, for the first time, the Mercatorian cartography, that is, the official map of the world originating in the colonial and imperial period. In the Peters projections the South is much more extended than its traditional image, showing how our image of the world corresponds to a distorted vision of its real proportions. Actually, the world map imposed by the colonial European countries is, still today, a political and economic image coming from the North and privileging the North. Yet, it is precisely when the artist seeks to establish the right order of things that paradoxically she takes distance from any attempt at precision. In Hatoum's artwork the earth is made visible through the different nuances created by the different qualities of the paper-pulp used – thin and transparent abaca paper forming the recessed continents and thick white cotton for the surrounding areas: nothing but a shadow, a quite insubstantial shape, a hardly perceptible drawing, a light mould of an absent body, of a migrant. A connection between geography and biography opens up here: the historical and ideological marginalization of the south of the world is interlaced with the processes of migration and the bodies of the migrants themselves. *Projection*, for instance, is reminiscent of some antecedent artworks where the artist "projects" herself through the traces of her body: in *Skin, Nail and Hair* (2003), *Hair Drawing* (2003) and *Blood Drawing* (2003), the artist impresses her skin, blood, hair, nails into the paper-pulp of what can be considered her self-portraits. She announces in a way the aesthetics and technique of her maps, unfolding through fullness and voids, the rough materiality and the fragile indeterminacy of the trace, as a presence that affirms herself defiantly through her losses, her remains, her non-conform, imprecise identity. Recalling the feminist "politics of location" and the observations of the Palestinian philosopher Elias Sanbar, it is possible to think of both Hatoum's maps and self-portraits as figures of a situated, material, yet becoming identity (Sanbar 2004) where a political and existential agency, a form of resistance to the threat of appropriation, erasure and absence is inscribed. Here any pretention to neatly define the borders of both the self and the world, any attempt to possess them, is destined to succumb to the limits of the recognizable and appropriable.

What Hatoum seems to propose is an "uprooted geography" whose disorienting maps can also be considered as "memory acts". They directly recall the existing maps of knowledge and power established by the cultural and political economy of Occidental past and present colonialisms, and question their violent maintenance of "centre" and "peripheries", hegemonic and subaltern areas, "First" and "Third" worlds. Hatoum produces a counter-geography of estrangement that undoes and continually redefines this persisting cartography of power. Another example working bluntly across and along the "struggle over geography" and its contested territories is the installation *3-D Cities* (2008–9) where printed maps of cities present geometrical cuts forming paper depressions and elevations, similar to roses or cones. But any association with beauty, choreography or playfulness results inappropriate, even disquieting, when, at a closer look, it is possible to see that the maps refer to Beirut, Kabul and Baghdad. Those cuts are more likely signs left by war, signs of violence.

Against the modern cartography of differentiated powers, Hatoum's maps create zones of ontological slippage, time-space interlacements, bonds between distance and proximity, personal and collective memories. Interrogating our position, our established procedures of recognition and definitions, the artist draws us into an alternative critical heterotopic space (Foucault [1967]). Here, overcoming barriers, borders, enclosures, divisions in favour of traces, signs, folds and unpredictable currents, we are propelled into the emergence of another challenging configuration.

Emily Jacir's Reconfigured Properties and Identities

The possibility of questioning institutional, historical and cultural borders of property, heritage and belonging is the challenge posed by the Palestinian artist Emily Jacir. Born and raised in Haifa, then living and working (as both an artist and scholar) between Palestine, the US (mainly New York) and Europe (where she spent part of her adolescence, attending high school in Rome), Jacir rearticulates the experience of diaspora. The emergent space and interpretive frame of the diaspora is rooted not only in older structures of power, but also in the experience of vulnerable minorities and the conditions of refugee camps, detention centres and invisible economies of the advanced world. Moreover, as Hall suggests, the idea of the diaspora questions the notions of a cultural origin, of roots and authenticity. Diaspora is where the politics of gender, class and race form together a new, powerful and unstable articulation that does not provide easy answers, but raises "new questions, which proliferate across older frames of thought, social engagement and political activity" (Hall 2012). Jacir's art is based on a diverse range of artistic languages and means, above all photography, video and installation, often set outside museum walls, in public spaces, and characterised by a direct involvement of the audience. Her artistic pieces can be more appropriately defined as critical public interventions or collective processes, based on participation, recollection, radical challenge and acting desire:

> With one foot in the United States and Italy and another firmly planted in Palestine, Emily Jacir navigates differing but related spheres. Her life in the United States dovetails with her life in Ramallah. Both are examples of living in the bellies of beasts, but Ramallah is where her soul is nourished. Between these and other spheres, Jacir follows an infectious credo never to negotiate against herself. Most importantly, Jacir recognizes when an audience is on the verge of becoming transformed and has consistently offered to cross those boundaries with them, always with the anticipation of advancing to the next challenge.
>
> (Bittar 2009, 149)

Significantly, the artist has often been criticised, and even censored, by institutional museums, galleries and art fairs, as it happened with her work, *Stazione*. This is the project of a public work commissioned in 2009 for a collateral event within the Venice Biennial, "Palestine c/o Venice" and then concealed by the municipality without giving any official reason (the unofficial one was to avoid a provocation of the islamophobic and arabophobic anxiety supposedly afflicting the Venetian population). The "incriminated" work consisted of a juxtaposition of the Italian names of the Vaporetto stations with their Arabic translation thus forming a multilingual line of transport across the city, which evokes the ancient common heritage between Venice, Italy, and the Arab world, based on migration and sea-crossings. The word *arsenale* itself, that is the place that hosts the Biennial main exhibition, comes from the Arabic *dar al-sina'a* (factory). Yet, Jacir provided a brochure (in Arabic, Italian and English) that was distributed around Venice. In addition to a map indicating where her translations were located, this pamphlet contained a summary of the historical influence of the Arab world on Venice since the sixteenth century, in terms not only of trade but also of cultural and scientific exchange.

Similarly, irrupting into the monolithic domain of nationalism constructed on silenced histories, Jacir's practice of intersection on the margin of institutional recognition intervenes, again, with her last installation, *Via Crucis*, in Milan, in the Catholic church of San Raffaele (Fig. 3.1). Here the exploration of an Arab Italy touches upon a mixed belonging of religious traditions and linguistic territory: "For me Arabic language is like a Latin dialect, or the Sicilian language, or the Arberesh". They are both articulated through the sense of "an impossible situatedness" (Demos 2003, 68) recalling the Palestinian condition. In this installation the artist reproduces the writing of the fourteen Stations of the Cross on round aluminium plates, seven of which are in Arabic and the rest in Italian. There are also some objects evoking what can be referred to as a "Palestinian via Crucis", recalling both the colonial siege and the religious worship in Jerusalem: barbed wire, suitcases, keys of expropriated homes, bullets, a traditional female dress. Other objects, such as fragments of a boat, pictures and nets, are from Lampedusa, gathered by the artist during her residence on the island. They concur to translate the different and yet interlaced narratives of migration, exile and belonging, reconnecting the city to the island, the urban heritage to the migrant memories of the sea. Other works or processes activated by Jacir are informed provocatively by this aesthetics of contrasts including personal and historical narratives that transcend the limits of place and time, and where the public is able to test the meaning of history and memory.

Jacir's art can be also defined as an aesthetics of contrasts, including personal and historical narratives that transcend the limits of place and time. Within her participative experiments, the public is able to test the meaning of history and memory. *Sexy Semite*, a wild guerrilla piece, was enacted each year from 2000 to 2002 before finally catching the attention of the press. Jacir and sixty Palestinians contributed ads to the personal section of the US newspaper *Village Voice,* seeking romantic liaisons with Jewish readers. They invited them to marry

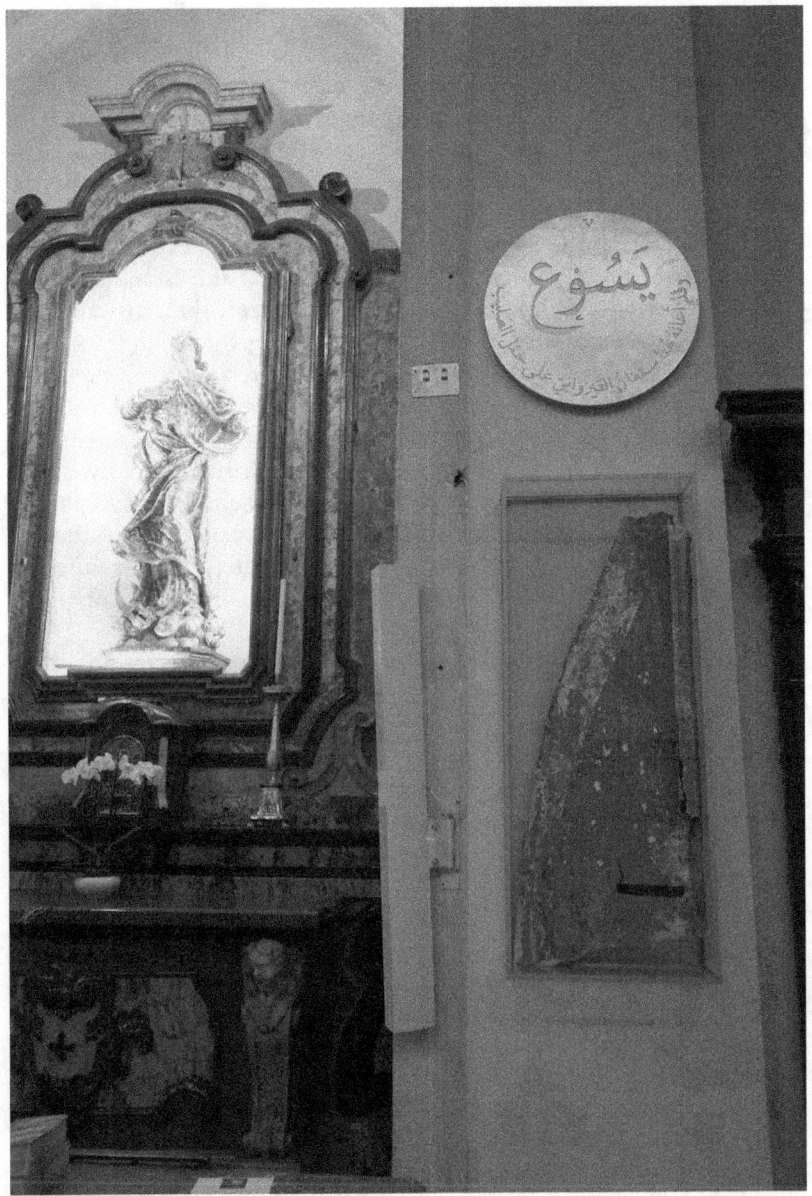

Figure 3.1 Emily Jacir, *Via Crucis: Station V (Simon of Cyrene Helps Jesus to Carry His Cross)*, 2013–16. Permanent installation at the Church of San Raffaele, Milan. Commissioned by Artache.

© Emily Jacir. Courtesy of the artist

Palestinians, thereby enabling them to return to Palestine using the Israeli "law of return". Another example, also employing a democratic process, is the haunting and incomplete piece, *Memorial to 418 Palestinian Villages which were Destroyed, Depopulated and Occupied by Israel in 1948* (2002). Jacir invited over 140 people to embroider the fabric of a tent with the names of the 418 towns and villages that were destroyed. The piece is a humble monument dedicated to the history of the occlusion of the Palestinian population and the expropriation of the land as a direct consequence of the birth of the Israeli state. In stark contrast to the classic image of a monument, the artist entrusts her desire to memorialise to a UN-issued refugee tent and a collective yet intimate practice of remembering and reconstruction. Jacir's *Memorial* documents a three-month community-based work, involving artists, activists, journalists or simply residents of the area near her studio in New York. Other people were spiritually involved: the 780,000 Palestinian refugees dispersed across the continents as part of the massive diaspora produced by the Israeli invasion and testimony to a progressing history of ruins, yet to be narrated. Emblematically, the work of sewing the names is left expressly incomplete (Kravagna, Menick and Said 2004).

In 2003 Jacir invented another brilliant participative action which gave her international recognition: *Where We Come From* (Fig. 3.2). In this intervention the artist performed the role of a humble servant to disenfranchised Palestinians, particularly those within Israeli-occupied lands. The work is thus based on the desire for what is systematically impeded or even denied, that is the free movement from one country to the other or within the Palestinians' own territory. Like a genie, having a US passport, Jacir carried out thirty wishes that came from individual Palestinians in the diaspora who could not fulfil their desires due to their disenfranchisement and the travel restrictions imposed by Israel. The work was also inspired by the question we are always asked at the borders: "Did someone give you something to carry?" The action proceeded then in an installation of photographs testifying to the action of the artist, each one accompanied by captions about the desire to which the image referred, thus articulating the "banality of exile" (Demos 2003, 70) through a continuous passage from image to words. Jacir's work can be considered an archive of desires, wherein is inscribed the paradox of their impossibility, the fact of being simultaneously accomplished and impeded, realised and denied. Viewers of *Where We Come From* became engaged witnesses to the inner workings of the Israeli occupation, its illogic and inhumanity.

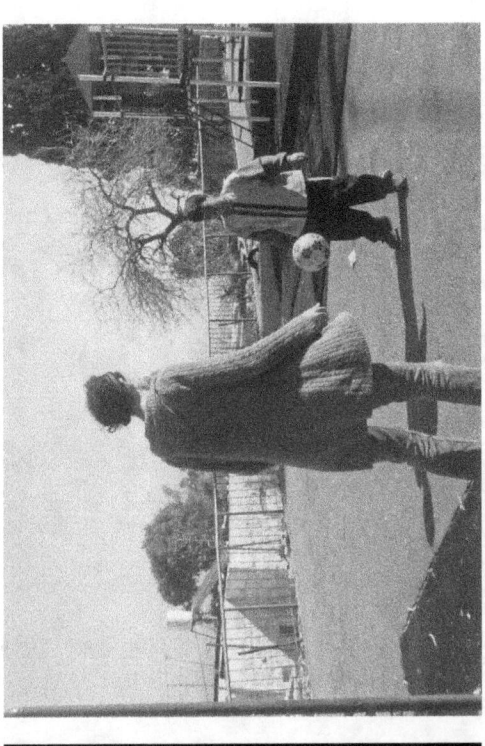

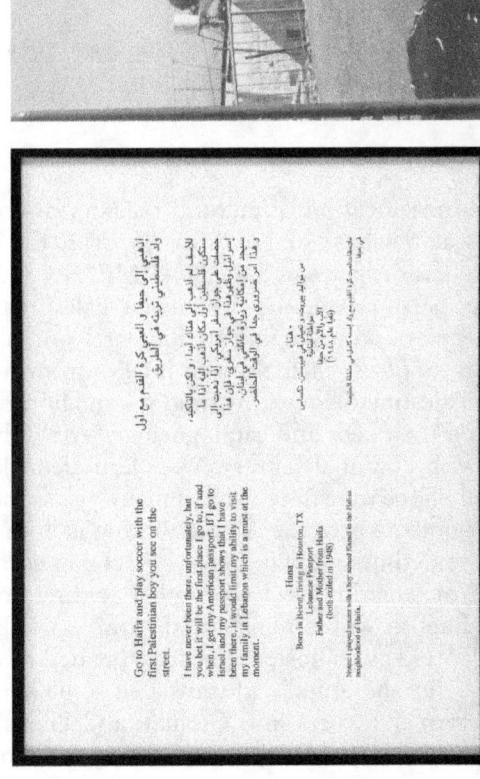

Figure 3.2 Emily Jacir, *Hana*, detail of *Where We Come From*. American passport, 30 texts, 32 C-prints, 1 video, 2001–3.
© Emily Jacir. Courtesy of the artist and Alexander and Bonin Gallery, New York

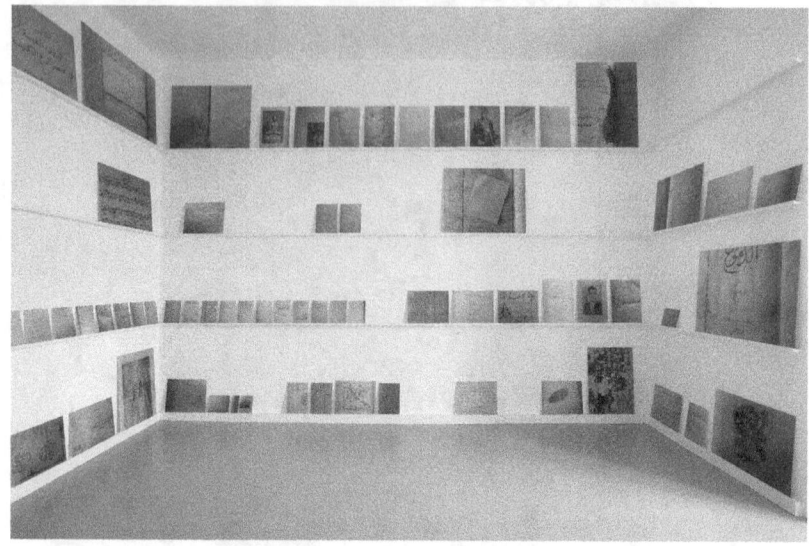

Figure 3.3 Emily Jacir, *ex libris*. Installation, public project and book, 2010–12.
Photo: Roman März, dOCUMENTA (13), 2012. © Emily Jacir. Courtesy of the artist and Alexander and Bonin Gallery, New York

The idea of a de-museification of cultural memory and decolonisation of archive is at the base of Jacir's *ex libris* (2012; Fig. 3.3), a photographic installation presented at dOCUMENTA (13), where she created a kind of personal museum from some Palestinian literary remains: history, memory and belonging are intimately interconnected and interrogated. In *ex libris*, Jacir showed images from more than 30,000 books from Palestinian homes, institutions and libraries looted by Israel in 1948 and then kept and catalogued as "AP" (abandoned property) in the Jewish National Library, West Jerusalem. Jacir took pictures with her cell phone over the course of many visits. She showed the pages of those books, where the Arabic writing is both in hand-written and typed, sometimes clear in bold characters and elsewhere almost disappeared or superimposed with other writing and hardly legible. Sometimes English words mingle with Arab ones. In Kassel, where dOCUMENTA (13) was hosted, the artist created a register of the traces and fragments she found and translated some handwritten inscriptions of the former owners into German and English, exhibiting them on billboards, in public spaces, weaving a dialogue with history and place. *Ex libris*, in fact, takes place in the Zwehrenturm, the area of the Fridericiarum Museum where manuscripts were stored and which survived the 1941 American bombing that destroyed other volumes kept in the museum library. Jacir also concentrated on the post-war period when the region of Hessel–Kassel was occupied by American forces. Here, the Offenbach Archival Depot, which hosted the books and manuscripts looted by the Nazis, instituted a process of restitution, the largest in a US zone up until then. Interlacing past and present experiences of siege and destruction (perpetuated by the United States and Israel) and superseding the borders of different histories and geographies (North America, central Europe, the Middle East), the artist appears to re-actualise the process of restitution, giving it a disruptive meaning that questions the very idea of ownership. The Palestinian books that were once brutally appropriated are now registered in a public vision and space, through a creative gesture that renders them unappropriable and uncontainable.

AP 3852 is a work directly connected to *ex libris*. It is a mural on a New York building, which reports a phrase in Arabic and its English translation drawn from a Palestinian book stored in the Jerusalem Library and catalogued as AP 3852. A looted book is appropriated, opportunistically labelled as abandoned property and archived as an anonymous object, whose identity is now reduced to the numbers and letters indicating its location. The private constellation of places, stories, people, memories linked to the book are thus brutally erased. Reversing the colonial paradigm of negation and subtraction that regulates the Zionist necropolitics, Jacir once again gives to the neglected memory a public, open, amplified dimension, turning the abandoned property into a reappropriated and freed privacy. The 8 by 17 metre mural in New York claims in various languages: "This book belongs to its owner, Fathallah Saad. He bought it with his own money, at the beginning of March 1982."

What these artworks produce is not simply a recuperation of what was lost, but the transformation of the loss into the possibility of a power that goes beyond colonial power towards a different recollection that activates memory as difference. Material and cultural heritage are here an open question, evoking Stuart Hall's invitation to reimagine the borders of national property (2002). A desire for recognition, restitution and emancipation that seems to pervade Jacir's art assumes the artist's personal sphere and biographical positionings as critical instruments, interlacing and simultaneously interrogating the public and the private, the personal and the collective, the distant and the closed, the private and the common.

Kader Attia's and Walid Raad's Reappropriations

An aesthetics concerning questions of material and cultural heritage is also what the Berlin-based French–Algerian artist Kader Attia proposes, exploring ideas and practices of reappropriation and reparation as processes of critical resistance and othering: for example, the installation *Repair: From Occidental to Extra-Occidental Cultures* (2012; Fig. 3.4). Shown at dOCUMENTA (13), this artwork brings us directly into a decomposed archive. Actually it presents itself as a sort of fragmented and random collection of objects coming from the past and elsewhere, gathered to form a subterranean and silent dialogue amongst themselves, where the temporal and spatial coordinates of their belonging and provenance interlace and multiply. Attia's work shows a series of different objects and images from some ex-colonised African countries and Europe, mainly tracing back to the colonial era and the interwar period. Collected by the artist over

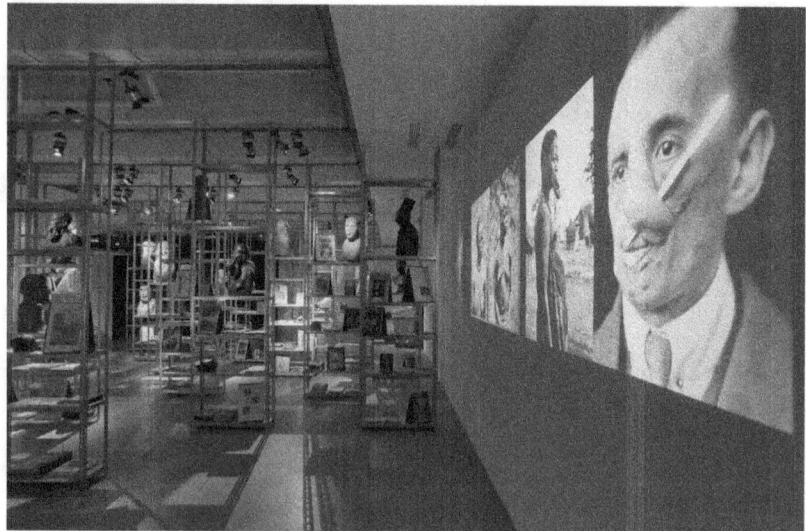

Figure 3.4 Kader Attia, *Repair: From Occidental to Extra-Occidental Cultures*. Mixed-media installation: view of installation at Museum Fridericianum, Kassel, 2012. Commissioned and produced by dOCUMENTA (13) with the support and courtesy of the artist, Galleria Continua, Galerie Nagel Draxler and Galerie Krinzinger; further support by Fondation nationale des arts graphiques et plastiques, France. Photo: Roman März.

fifteen years, the aesthetic material exhibited is highly varied: from traditional wooden sculptures from Dakar and Senegal to marble ones from Carrara, Italy. Alongside these are old newspapers, books, magazines, original photographs, and African artefacts, photocopies, metallic objects; some of them show signs of repair, other have been reconstructed with pieces of other objects: from vitrines and mestizo objects (objects of extra-Occidental cultures integrating an element of Occidental cultures) to trench art (objects made by soldiers in the trenches during the First World War using cartridges and artillery shells). In the passage from the private archive to the public one of the art fair, these repaired and presumably fragile objects keep something intimate and private with them, something reluctant to exhibition, a sort of shame for exposition or an unpresentability. Disposed on iron shelves, similar to those used for storage, and in wooden showcases similar to those used in museums, and fixed with big screws and nails, the objects seem to be caught and kept rather than simply shown.

A slide show is also part of Attia's installation, it displays images of the so-called *gueules cassées*, the Great War veterans, thus named because of their physical damage, especially to their faces, where the signs of massive surgical interventions are irreparably evident. Enlisted both in the European homeland and its African colonies, these mutilated combatants recalled the absurd violence exercised by men on other men: the monstrosity of both war and colonisation. Reduced to their corporeal wounds, they were identified as "broken faces" and were allowed little social visibility or historical recognition. In France, for example, they were assigned by the French government a house some 40 kilometres from Paris and often excluded from public commemorations of the war. Their status as damaged survivors, as disfigured individuals, being damaged but not yet dead, made them reminders of an open wound and unrepaired debt to/from the past, which also involved the colonised "extra-Occidental" combatants and their tribute paid to the European coloniser. This prevented them being hailed as "heroes" of the homeland.

So, what do the images of those broken faces say? Is the broken face slideshow in Attia's *Repair* a "resurrection", activating a form of historical restitution? Is this an attempt to recompose a lacking historical mosaic with the inclusion of the missing parts? Maybe there is all of this at play in this installation, but also even more than this, especially if one considers that the work evokes not so much a sense of historical pacification and reconciliation as a sense of disturbance and a problematisation of any attempt to produce a simple historical account.

This is evident in the juxtaposition of objects of beauty like the African and Italian sculptures with war objects and in between the repaired artefacts and images of dismembered bodies. Actually what can, at first glance, be perceived as being juxtaposed displays a dynamic of cultural interplay, realised "as a life continuum for the so-to-speak 'dead' archive":[3] that is, on the basis of the visual archives of the First World War and the ethnographic archives of the nineteenth century. A transcultural repository of mutilations, of bodies considered as "imperfect" from the European look based on an idea of beauty that is inseparable from that of integrity.

In the same way that the disfigured bodies recall the violence of war, so too are the displayed objects in radical opposition to the image of the auratic objects of museum display. They are repaired, sutured, stitched, recomposed with other remains, they seem to be simultaneously within and beyond the museographic spectacle, so hybrid and altered are they. Attia's installation activates a disruptive encounter with a repressed historical narration and materiality, confronting the spectator with the possibility of repair as an exercise in cultural reappropriation. The "reparations" shown by Kader Attia can be read as forms of cultural reappropriation: "signs of resistance against a modern world that has utterly failed to understand the underlying motivations of the non-Western subject" (Attia 2013). What Kader Attia put in play is also a reappropriation of those "dead archives" lying at the heart of the modern European identity. A reappropriation based on proximity and affect, the objects here are physical, touchable and above all approachable. They reduce the distance imposed by the conventional museum display. What opens up here is the possibility of touching, of coming into contact or meeting something different, strange, "othered", contaminated, beyond perfection, integration and authenticity. In the interstices of a dismembered and re-membered identity, we can hear, as Attia says, "many voices, a cacophony of always already reiteratively intra-acting stories. These are entangled tales. Each is diffractively threaded through and enfolded in the other. Is that not in the nature of touching?" (2013). Establishing a contact with these objects implies a radical historical and identitarian interrogation. Attia's installation activates a disruptive encounter with a repressed historical narration and materiality, confronting the spectator with the possibility of repair as an exercise in cultural reappropriation, and above all with

3 https://universes.art/nafas/articles/2013/kader-attia-kw.

the problematic existence of what Tarek Elhaik defines as "incurable images" of history (2014).

Alternative European archives can also be found in Senegal, as shown by Attia's work *Indépendance Tchao* (2014), showed at the Dakar biennial (Fig. 3.5). It is inspired by the Independence Hotel, an

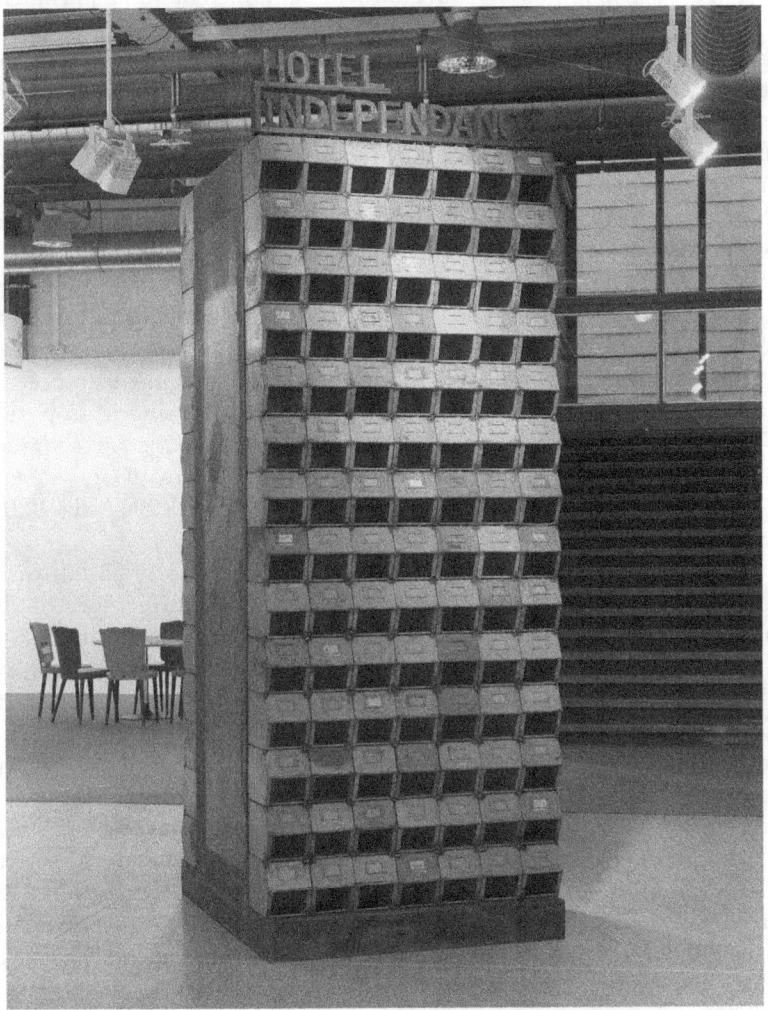

Figure 3.5 Kader Attia, *Indépendance Tchao*. Mixed media installation, 2014: view of installation at Art Basel, Basel, 2015. Photo: Simon Vogel.

© Kader Attia. Courtesy of the artist and Galerie Nagel Draxler

abandoned building in the centre of Dakar, what remains of a postcolonial nationalist project, now only to be looked at as an archaeologi-
cal museum piece. The artist proposes a reconfiguration of this edifice,
now become a memorial of oblivion, turning its architecture into an
archive made up of postcolonial remains. The installation reproduces
the hotel in miniature by using the little metal boxes of an archive,
which the artist has taken from another abandoned building in Algiers.
The artistic practice is here an exercise of historical reappropriation
through a work of salvage and reuse, critical recycling, demolition and
reconstruction, dismantling and collaging. This is both a deterritorialisation and territorialisation of a forgotten patrimony, a process where
damaged memory is repaired. Attia's art of contamination and regen-
eration touches both historical and human issues, and also concerns
the natural laws. It recognised in the process of repair a fundamental
principle of creation and renovation of the whole universe:

> Repair in the cultural sense of the word can apply to politics, the
> economy, art, and science, but it is above all on the continuum of
> extra-cultural activity. What we claim to control, for instance, by
> gathering information with the intention of reusing it, is purely
> an imitation of fundamental physical phenomena structuring an
> order of things that precedes and will succeed us as well.
>
> (Attia 2015)

Attia's aesthetics of repair recall the art of critical error and disturbing intervention of the Lebanese artist Walid Raad, member of the
photographic archive the Arab Image Foundation and founder of
the fictional collective the Altas Group, based like the artist in New
York and Beirut, and dedicated to the construction of an archive of the
Lebanese wars, delegitimising the conventional binary historiographical distinction between fiction and non-fiction.[4] Like all the artistic
examples analysed in this study, Raad's artworks are an invitation to
cross the border of a space (a map, an archive, an atlas) which is displacing, tricky, and at the same time, gentle, subtle, touching, affective.
In his 2006 photographic series, *We Decided to Let Them Say, "We
are Convinced", Twice*, Raad draws the landscapes of his native city,
Beirut. They are old photos taken by Raad when he was adolescent in
1982, during the Israeli invasion of the western part of the city, with

4 See www.theatlasgroup.org.

the aim of establishing through photographic means the closest proximity with the events:

> In the summer of 1982, I stood along with others in a parking lot across from my mother's apartment in East Beirut, and watched the Israeli land, air, and sea assault on West Beirut. The PLO along with their Lebanese and Syrian allies retaliated, as best they could. East Beirut welcomed the invasion, or so it seemed, and that much is certain. West Beirut resisted it, or so it seemed, and that much is certain. One day, my mother even accompanied me to the hills around Beirut to photograph the invading Israeli army stationed there. Soldiers rested their bodies and their weapons as they waited for their next orders to attack, retreat or stay put. I was 15 in 1982, and wanted to get as close as possible to the events, or as close as my newly acquired camera and lens permitted me that summer. This past year, I came upon my carefully preserved negatives from that time. I decided to look again.
>
> (We Find Wildness 2011)

After twenty-five years, the artist decided to go back to his negatives and look at them beyond his old, naive illusion of capturing reality. Now, images are enlarged, showing the traces of time – strips and scratches that remind to the wounds of the war – and of digital interventions in different colours: blue, green, pink. Somewhere in the same series, the colour intrusions have the shape of dots, points, little circles, made to camouflage and at the same time highlight the holes left by bullets on houses in Beirut.

The drawn landscape attesting to the memory of a trauma now withdraws, subtracting itself to a precise identification. What is this formal play with colours? Why this irreverent digital ghosting on the memory of a wound? The question has to do with touching and withdrawal as immediate effects of a defensive strategy from sorrow. This is a concept elaborated by the artist and writer Jalal Toufic (2009), who has deeply inspired Raad's work about the long wars and siege of Lebanon. Toufic explores the concept of a withdrawal of tradition past a surpassing disaster, that is, how a disaster can damage tradition. In particular, the artworks undergo a process of withdrawal, they become being perceived as damaged, destroyed, not disposable to vision. The material wound survives immaterially. Raad, in fact, says:

> The Lebanese wars of the past three decades affected Lebanon's residents physically and psychologically: from the hundred thousand

plus who were killed; to the two hundred thousand plus who were wounded; to the million plus who were displaced; to the even more who were psychologically traumatized. Needless to say, the wars also affected Lebanese cities, buildings and institutions. It is clear to me today that these wars also affected colours, lines, shapes and forms. Some of these were affected in a material way and, like burned books or razed monuments, are physically destroyed and lost forever. Others, like looted treasure or politically com- promised artworks, remain physically intact but are removed from view, possibly never to be seen again. And yet other colours, lines, shapes and forms, sensing the forthcoming danger, deploy defen- sive measures: they hide, take refuge, hibernate, camouflage and dissimulate.

(Raad 2007)

The camouflage or withdrawal is meant as a response to the danger of disappearance or as effect of the disappearance of reality itself, after a disaster. The landscape is irremediably touched, it reduces, deforms – it undergoes the "Alice effect", to put it in Deleuzian terms – overcomes the borders of the recognisable, confuses memory, both collective and personal, questions reality. For instance, in Raad's project dedicated to the art history of the Arab world, *Scratching on Things I Could Dis- avow*, the names of Lebanese artists, which Raad says he received tele- pathically from artists of the future, appear like white lines on ruined walls and sometimes, owing to some disturbances of the telepathic signals, the names have a mistake. The latter could be unobserved, above all by the non-Arabic-speaking public, if Raad did not empha- sise them with a spray of colour, since as Raad maintains, the artists of the future need colour. The use of colour, as well as that of deforma- tions and estrangement, becomes here a cultural and political practice, other than an aesthetic technique.

As happens with Attia's damaged objects, here the constant evoking of the conflict, of war and colonial violence mark an interruption in the enjoyment of an ideal and displayed aesthetic beauty, preserved and exposed in a well-curated space, anesthetised and seemingly immune from historical contingencies and the conflicts of contemporaneity. Emblematically, Raad explores the museum's cultural and financial system by processes reminding of decomposition, fragmentation, dis- section, and *mise en abyme*. *Scratching on Things I Could Disavow* displays silhouettes of museum doors and frames of different sizes and colour on white walls; entrances and images of empty museums; small- scale museums with miniature images of the artist's projects. Another component of the project is a tableau with luminescent writings and numbers referring to the invisible relations between art history, museum system, war industry, funds and investors, management and algorithms, and hoe that affects the value of art and the sense of history. Raad recalls the importance of considering memory as an interior landscape that is inextricably linked to a complex external one, with its social, cultural, geographical and historical differences. Memory is a hybrid, conflictual, critical landscape. Raad invites us to a critical negotiation with what Sharon Macdonald defines as a "difficult heritage" (2009) inscribed in the cultural memory and above all with the irreparable damage and the irrepressible aspects of every conflict, often silenced by the official versions of history. This aesthetic of border-crossing, tricky reports and historical reappropriation emerging from the Raad's Atlas Group could then be seen as a challenge to the too neat distinctions between reality and fiction, historical document and invention, representation and repression. This questions radically the myth of authenticity and linear, univocal historical narrations. The work, *Missing the Lebanese War* (1999), where "missing" stands for both desire and lack, is an emblematic example evoking the vicious circle where the desire to report and narrate bumps up constantly into the impossibility of it coming true.

What is ultimately damaged here is the archive, the museum and its power to enunciate and conserve, which is at the same time a power of exclusion and oblivion. This is often linked directly or indirectly to the dynamics of political and above all economic power that dominate the contemporary art world, as Raad shows when he underlines the big interest in art and the construction and foundation of new museums by Gulf sheiks. However, as he observes, the Metropolitan Museum of Art was also constructed by robber barons or "American sheiks" about one hundred years ago, thus moving the centre of modern art from Paris to New York (Raad 2009).

The aim here is not so much to recall attention to the undoubtedly interesting connivances between political power, market exigencies, financial disposability and contemporary art museums along with the manifold organic particles that sustain its system: directors, curators, collectors and influential critics. Attention is paid to how art, and in particular what can be defined as postcolonial art, can constitute a destabilising and uncomfortable external and internal component of this system, thus creating a short circuit, a constant menace of sabotage or, as Derrida would have it, a hostile supplement that breaches the frame, opening up to the chance of differences and the radical questioning it brings with it ([1978]). This breach does not simply concern the museum of contemporary art and the so-called art-system, but it invests also the traditional borders that separate art museums from ethnographic and historical museums or from natural history museums and science museums. The breach concerns the persisting bold walls of disciplines that such institutions produce and legitimate, their presumed autonomy and the Occidental humanist and nationalist basis on which they are founded. It is here, in the "othered" archives, where the postcolonial aesthetics transpose us that a possibility opens up to see, hear and experience alternative histories and memories, whose narrations are not reserved to the field of visual arts and art history but rather escape the closure of any disciplinary and singular narrative of time and space. This is how art offers "another way of telling", to put it in John Berger and Jean Mohr's words (1982), which is far from being like a neutral window on the world, a universal and distant gaze on reality, but rather a perspective with multiple shards of telling and understanding the world, a spectrum of voices and gazes from different bodies of experiences and lives.

References

Adolphs, Volker, 2004. "The Body and the World". In *Mona Hatoum*, ed. Christoph Heinrich. Ostfildern: Hatje Cranz Publishers.

Antoni, Janine, 1998. Interview with Mona Hatoum. *Bomb Magazine* 63. www.bombmagazine.org/articles/mona-hatoum.

Appadurai, Arjun, 1996. *Modernity at Large: Cultural Dimensions of Globalization*. New York and London: Routledge.

Attia, Kader, 2013. *Repair: Architecture, Reappropriation, and the Body Repaired*. http://kaderattia.de/repair-architecture-reappropriation-and-the-body-repaired.

Attia, Kader, 2015. "The Loop". *E-flux Journal* May–August: 1–6.

Bakhtin, Mikhail, [1965]. *Rabelais and His World*, trans. Helene Iswolsky. Bloomington: Indiana University Press, 1984.

Bal, Mieke, 1996. *Double Exposures: The Subject of Cultural Analysis*. New York and London: Routledge.

Barad, Karen, 2012. "On Touching: The Inhuman that Therefore I Am". *Differences: A Journal of Feminist Cultural Studies* 23/3: 206-23.

Barthes, Roland, 1975. *Roland Barthes par Roland Barthes*. Paris: Éditions du Seuil.

Baudrillard, Jean. 1987. *Forget Foucault*. New York: Columbia University.

Bennett, Tony, 1988. "The Exhibitionary Complex". *New Formations* 4: 73–102.

Berger, John, 1972. *Ways of Seeing*. London: Penguin Books.

Berger, John, 1991. *Keeping a Rendezvous*. London: Vintage.

Berger, John, and Jean Mohr, 1982. *Another Way of Telling*. New York, Vintage.

Bhabha, K. Homi, 1994. *The Location of Culture*. London and New York: Routledge.

Bhabha, K. Homi, 1996. "Unpacking my Library . . . Again". In *The Postcolonial Question: Common Skies, Divided Horizons*, ed. Iain Chambers and Lidia Curti. London and New York: Routledge.

Biemann, Ursula, 2014. "Egyptian Chemistry: From Postcolonial to Post-Humanist Matters". In *The Postcolonial Museum: The Arts of Memory and the Pressures of History*, ed. Iain Chambers et al. Farnham: Ashgate.

Bishop, Claire, 2012. *Artificial Hell: Participatory Art and the Politics of Participation*. London: Verso.

Bittar, Doris, 2009. "Crossing Boundaries". *Canvas: Art and Culture from the Middle East and Arab World* 5/2: 138–49.

Bodei, Remo, 2004. "Riflessioni su alcune premesse dell'arte interattiva" [Reflections on Some Premises of Interactive Art]. In *Arte tra azione e contemplazione* [Art between Action and Interaction], ed. Silvana Vassallo and Andreina Di Brino. Pisa: ETS.

Bourriaud, Nicolas, [1998]. *Relational Aesthetics*. Paris: Les Presses du Réel, 2002.

Braidotti, Rosi, 2006. *Transpositions: On Nomadic Ethics*. Cambridge: Polity Press.

Brown, Wendy, 2010. *Walled States, Waning Sovereignty*. Brooklyn, NY: Zone Books.

Butler, Judith, 1990. *Gender Trouble: Feminism and the Subversion of Identity*. London and New York: Routledge.

Butler, Judith, 2004. *Precarious Life: The Powers of Mourning and Violence*. London and New York: Verso.

Carotenuto, Silvana, 2012. "Arkè e vision femminile: una chora di lingua" [Arkè and Female Visions: A Chora of Language]. *Estetica: Studi e ricerche* 3: 101–16.

Chambers, Iain, 1997. *Migrancy, Culture, Identity*. London and New York: Routledge.

Chambers, Iain, 2008. *Mediterranean Crossings: The Politics of an Interrupted Modernity*. Durham, NC: Duke University Press.

Chambers, Iain, 2012. "Cultural Memories, Museums Spaces and Archiving". In *Museums in an Age of Migrations: Questions, Challenges, Perspectives*, ed. Luca Basso Peressut and Clelia Pozzi. Milan: Politecnico di Milano.

Chambers, Iain, Giulia Grechi and Mark Nash (eds) 2014. *The Ruined Archive*. Milan: Politecnico di Milano.

Chambers, Iain, et al. (eds) 2014. *The Postcolonial Museum: The Arts of Memory and the Pressures of History*. London: Routledge.

Chow, Rey, 1992. "Postmodern Automatons". In *Feminists Theorize the Political*, ed. Judith Butler and Joan Wallach Scott. London and New York: Routledge.

Cianelli, Alessandra, 2014a. *Il paese delle terre d'Oltremare* [The Land of the Overseas Territories]. www.ilpaesedelleterredoltremare.wordpress.com.

Cianelli, Alessandra, 2014b. *Parole che (si) nascondono* [Words that Hide / are Hidden]. In *Postcolonial Matters: Tra gesti politici e scritture poetiche* [Between Political Gestures and Poetical Writings], ed. Beatrice Ferrara and Alessandra Cianelli. Naples: Università degli Studi di Napoli "L'Orientale" .

Cixous, Hélène, 1976. "The Laugh of the Medusa". *Signs: Journal of Women in Culture and Society* 1/4: 875–93.

Collettivo Askavusa n.d. *Porto M*. https://askavusa.wordpress.com/con-gli-oggetti/porto-m.

Curti, Lidia, 2004. *La voce dell'altra*. Rome: Meltemi.

Curti, Lidia, 2010. "Migrant Identities from the Mediterranean: A Southern Italian Vista". *California Italian Studies Journal* 1/1: 1–18.

Curti, Lidia, 2012. "Beyond White Walls". In *Cultural Memory, Migrating Modernities and Museum Practices*, ed. Beatrice Ferrara. Milan: Politecnico di Milano.

Deleuze, Gilles, [1969]. *The Logic of Sense*. New York: Columbia University Press, 1990.

Deleuze, Gilles, and Félix Guattari [1980]. *A Thousand Plateaus: Capitalism and Schizophrenia*. London and New York: Continuum, 1987.

Demos, T. J., 2003. "Desire in Diaspora: Emily Jacir". *Art Journal* 62/4: 68–79.

Derrida, Jacques, [1978]. *The Truth in Painting*. Chicago: University of Chicago Press, 1987.

Derrida, Jacques, 1995. *Archive Fever: A Freudian Impression*, trans. Eric Prenowitz. Chicago and London: University of Chicago Press.

Derrida, Jacques, 1998. *Monolingualism of the Other, or The Prothesis of Origin*, trans. Patrick Mensah. Stanford, CA: Stanford University Press.

De Zegher, Catherine, 1996. "Introduction: Inside the Visible". In *Inside the Visible:An Elliptical Traverse of 20th Century Art in, of, and from the Feminine*. Boston: Institute of Contemporary Arts.

Diagne, Souleymane Bachir, 2013. "On the Postcolonial and the Universal?" *Rue Descartes* 78/2: 7–18.

Djebar, Assia, [1980]. *Women of Algiers in Their Apartment*. Charlottesville: University Press of Virginia, 1999.

Djebar, Assia, [1996]. *Le Blanc de l'Algérie* [Algerian White]. Paris: LGF-Livre de Poche, 2002.

Dominijanni, Ida, 2015. "Muri d'impotenza" [Walls of Impotance]. *Internazionale* 28 Aug. www.internazionale.it/opinione/ida-dominijanni/2015/08/28/muri-impotenza-migranti-unione-europea.

Elhaik, Tarek, 2014. "The Incurable Image: Curation and Repetition on a Tricontinental Scene". In *The Postcolonial Museum: The Arts of Memories and the Pressures of History*, ed. Iain Chambers et al. London: Routledge.

Ettinger, Bracha, 1993. *Matrix, Halal(a)-Lapsus: Notes on Paintings 1985–1992*. Oxford: Museum of Modern Art.

Ettinger, Bracha, 2006. *The Matrixial Borderspace*. Minneapolis: University of Minnesota Press.

Fanon, Franz, [1952]. *Black Skin, White Masks*. New York: Grove Press, 2008.

Ferrara, Beatrice, (ed.) 2012. *Cultural Memory, Migrating Modernities and Museum Practices*. Milan: Politecnico di Milano.

Foucault, Michel, [1967]. "Of Other Spaces". *Diacritics* 16/1 (1986): 22–7.

Fusco, Coco, 2004. "Questioning the Frame: Thoughts about Maps and Spatial Logic in the Global Present". *In These Times* 16 Dec. www.inthesetimes.com/article/1750.

Gilroy, Paul, 1987. *There Ain't No Black in the Union Jack: The Cultural Politics of Race and Nation*. London: Hutchinson.

Gilroy, Paul, 1993. *The Black Atlantic: Modernity and Double Consciousness*. London and New York: Verso.

Glissant, Édouard, [1990]. *Poetics of Relation*. Ann Arbor: University of Michigan Press. 1997.

Golding, Viv, 2013. "Museums, Poetics and Affect". *Feminist Review* 104/1: 80–99.

Gramsci, Antonio, [1948–51]. *The Southern Question*, trans. Pasquale Verdicchio. Toronto: Guernica Editions, 2005.

Grosz, Elizabeth, 2005. *Time Travels: Feminism, Nature, Power*. Durham, NC: Duke University Press.

Grosz, Elizabeth, 2008. *Chaos, Territory, Art: Deleuze and the Framing of the Earth*. New York: Columbia University Press.

Gubar, Susan, 1986. "'The Blank Page' and the Issue of Female Creativity". In *New Feminist Criticism*, ed. Elaine Showalter. London: Virago Press.

Hall, Stuart, 2001. "Museums of Modern Art and the End of History." In *Annotations 6: Modernity and Difference*, ed. Stuart Hall and Sarat Maharaj. London: INIVA.

Hall, Stuart, 2002. "Whose Heritage? Unsettling 'The Heritage', Re-imagining the Post-Nation." In *The Third Text Reader on Art, Culture, and Theory*, ed. Rashid Araeen, Sean Cubitt and Ziauddin Sardar. London: Continuum.

Hall, Stuart, 2012. "Avtar Brah's Cartographies: Moment, Method, Meaning". *Feminist Review* 100: 27–38.

Hall, Stuart, and Jessica Evans (eds) 1999. *Visual Culture: The Reader*. London: Sage.

Haraway, Donna, 1991. *Simians, Cyborg and Women: The Reinvention of Nature*. London and New York: Routledge.

Haraway, Donna, 2007. *When Species Meet*. Minneapolis: University of Minnesota Press.

Haraway, Donna, 2016. *Staying with the Trouble: Making Kin in the Chthulucene*. Durham, NC, and London: Duke University Press.

hooks, bell, 1990. "Postmodern Blackness". In *Yearning: Race, Gender and Cultural Politics*. Toronto: Between the Lines.

Hooper-Greenhill, Eilean, 2000. *Museums and the Interpretation of Visual Culture*. London: Routledge.

Horden, Peregrine, et al. 2006. "The Mediterranean and the 'New Thalassology'". *American Historical Review* 111(3): 722–40.

Irigaray, Luce, 2004. *Key Writings*. London and New York: Continuum.

Jones, Amelia, 1998. *Body Art / Performing the Subject*. Minneapolis: University of Minnesota Press.

Kaplan, Caren, and Inderpal Grewal (eds) 1994. *Scattered Hegemonies: Postmodernity and Transnational Feminist Practices*. Minneapolis: University of Minnesota Press.

Khanna, Ranjana, 2008. *Algeria Cuts: Women and Representation: 1860 to the Present*. Stanford, CA: Stanford University Press.

Krauss, Rosalind, 1999. *Bachelors*. Cambridge, MA: MIT Press.

Kravagna, Christian, John Menick and Edward Said 2004. *Emily Jacir: Belongings. Works: 1998–2003*. Vienna: Folio.

Kristeva, Julia, 1982. *Powers of Horror: An Essay on Abjection*, trans. Leon Samuel Roudiez. New York: Columbia University Press.

Kristeva, Julia, [1988]. *Strangers to Ourselves*. New York: Columbia University Press, 1991.

Macdonald, Sharon, 2009. *Difficult Heritage: Negotiating the Nazi Past in Nuremberg and Beyond*. London and New York: Routledge.

McGonagle, Joseph, 2007. "An Interstitial Intimacy: Renegotiating the Public and the Private in the Work of Zineb Sedira". *French Cultural Studies* 18/2: 219–35.

Mbembe, Achille, 2008. "What is Postcolonial Thinking?", *Eurozine* 12. www.eurozine.com/articles/2008-01-09-mbembe-en.html.

Mbembe, Achille, 2017. *Critique of Black Reason*, trans Laurent Dubois. Durham: Duke University Press.

Mezzadra, Sandro, 2008. *La condizione postcoloniale: Storia e politica nel presente globale* [The Postcolonial Condition: History and Politics of the Global Present]. Verona: Ombre Corte.

Minh-ha, Trinh T., 1992. "Cotton and Iron". In *Out There: Marginalization and Contemporary Cultures*, ed. Russell Ferguson et al. Cambridge, MA: MIT Press.

Minh-ha, Trinh T., 2005. *The Digital Film Event*. New York and London: Routledge.

Mirzoeff, Nicholas, (ed.) 1998. *The Visual Culture Reader*. London and New York: Routledge.

Mirzoeff, Nicholas, 1999. *An Introduction to Visual Culture*. London and New York: Routledge.

Moore, Lindsey, 2008. *Arab, Muslim, Woman: Voice and Vision in Postcolonial Literature and Film*. London and New York: Routledge.

Moraga, Cherrìe, 2000. *Loving in the War Years*. Brooklyn, NY: South End Press.

Nietzsche, Friedrich, [1888]. *Ecce Homo: Nietzsche's Autobiography*. Basingstoke: Macmillan, 1911.

Parker, Rozsika, 2010. *The Subversive Stitch: Embroidery and the Making of the Feminine*. London and New York: I.B. Tauris.

Phelan, Peggy, 1993. *Unmarked: The Politics of Performance*. New York: Routledge.

Philippi, Desa, 1999. "Mona Hatoum: Some Any No Every Body." In *Inside the Visible*, ed. Catherine de Zegher. Boston, MA: MIT Press.

Philo, Chris, 2000. "Foucault's Geography". In *Thinking Space*, ed. Mike Crang and Nigel Thrift. London and New York: Routledge.

Pollock, Griselda, 1999. *Differencing the Canon: Feminist Desire and the Writing of Art's Histories*. New York: Routledge.

Pratt, Mary Louise, 1991. "Arts of the Contact Zone". *Profession*: 33–40.

Preciado, Paul B., 2013. *Testo Junkie: Sex, Drugs, and Biopolitics in the Pharmacopornographic Era*. New York: Feminist Press.

Puar, Jasbir, 2007. *Terrorist Assemblages: Homonationalisms in Queer Times*. Durham, NC: Duke University Press.

Raad, Walid, 2007. *Scratching on Things I Could Disavow: Some Essays From the Atlas Group Project*. Lisbon: Culturgest Gallery.

Rich, Adrienne, 1985. "Notes Towards a Politics of Location". In *Women, Feminist Identity, and Society in the 1980's: Selected Papers*, ed. Myriam Diaz-Diocaretz and Iris M. Zavala. Amsterdam: John Benjamins Publishing.

Rivera Magos, Alessandro, 2009. "Musei e postcolonialismo, ridare voce ai 'subalterni': Interivsta ad Iain Chambers", *Babelmed*. http://ita.babelmed.net/cultura-e-societa/36-mediterraneo/4474-musei-e-postcolonialismo-ridare-voce-ai-subalterni.html.

Rogoff, Irit, 2000. *Terra Infirma: Geography's Visual Culture*. London and New York: Routledge.

Said, Edward, 2000a. "The Art of Displacement: Mona Hatoum's Logic of Irreconcilables". In *Mona Hatoum: The Entire World as a Foreign Land*, ed. Edward Said and Sheena Wagstaff. London: Tate Gallery Publishing.

Said, Edward, 2000b. *Reflexions on Exile and Other Essays*. Cambridge, MA.: Havard University Press

Sanbar, Elias, 2004. *Figures du Palestinien: Identité des origins, identité de devenir*. Paris: Gallimard.

Sedira, Zineb, n.d. *Mother Tongue*. Luxonline. http://www.luxonline.org.uk/artists/zineb_sedira/mother_tongue.html.

Senellart, Michel, (ed.) 2007. *Michel Foucault:Security, Territory, Population*, trans. Graham Burchell. New York: Palgrave Macmillan.

Smith, Sidonie, 1993. *Subjectivity, Identity and the Body*. Bloomington: Indiana University Press.

Smith, Sidonie, and Julia Watson (eds) 2002. "Introduction". In *Interfaces: Women, Autobiography, Image, Performance*. Ann Arbor: University of Michigan Press.

Sossi, Federica, 2006. *Migrare: Spazi di confinamento e strategie di esistenza*. Milan: Il Saggiatore.

Spivak, Gayatri C., 1988. "Can the Subaltern Speak?" In *Marxism and the Interpretation of Culture*, ed. Cary Nelson and Lawrence Grossberg. Urbana and Chicago: University of Illinois Press.

Spivak, Gayatri C., 1999. *A Critique of Post-Colonial Reason: Toward a History of the Vanishing Present*. Cambridge, MA: Harvard University Press.

Spinoza, Baruch, [1677]. *Ethics*, trans. W. H. White. Los Angeles: Moonrise Press, 2017.

Stanton, Domna, 1984. "Autogynography: Is the Subject Different?" in *The Female Autograph*. New York: New York Literary Forum.

Toufic, Jalal, 2009. *The Withdrawal of Tradition Past a Surpassing Disaster.* Berkeley, CA: Forthcoming Books.

Walcott, Derek 1990. *Omeros.* New York: Farrar, Straus & Giroux.

Walters, William, 2004. "Secure Borders, Safe Haven, Domopolitics". *Citizenship Studies* 8: 237–60.

We Find Wildness 2011. *The Atlas Group.* www.we-find-wildness.com/2011/11/the-atlas-group.

Index

Headings in italics indicate the title of an artwork or publication. Page numbers followed by n refer to information in a note.

For Product Safety Concerns and Information please contact our EU
representative GPSR@taylorandfrancis.com
Taylor & Francis Verlag GmbH, Kaufingerstraße 24, 80331 München, Germany